Making *the* Best *of* STRESS

How Life's Hassles Can Form the Fruit of the Spirit

Mark R. McMinn

InterVarsity Press

Downers Grove, Illinois

©1996 by Mark R. McMinn

InterVarsity Press® is the book-publishing division of InterVarsity Christian Fellowship®, a student movement active on campus at hundreds of universities, colleges and schools of nursing in the United States of America, and a member movement of the International Fellowship of Evangelical Students. For information about local and regional activities, write Public Relations Dept., InterVarsity Christian Fellowship, 6400 Schroeder Rd., P.O. Box 7895, Madison, WI 53707-7895.

Scripture quotations, unless otherwise noted, are from the New Revised Standard Version of the Bible, copyright 1989 by the Division of Christian Education of the National Council of the Churches of Christ in the USA. Used by permission. All rights reserved.

Cover photograph: Jerry Alexander/Tony Stone Images

ISBN 0-8308-1981-9

Printed in the United States of America ∞

Library of Congress Cataloging-in-Publication Data

McMinn, Mark R.
   Making the best of stress: how life's hassles can form the fruit
of the Spirit/Mark R. McMinn.
       p.   cm.
   Includes bibliographical references.
   ISBN 0-8308-1981-9 (paper: alk. paper)
   1. Christian life.   2. Stress (Psychology)—Religious aspects—
Christianity.   I. Title.
BV4501.2.M43654   1996
248.4—dc20   95-49667
                                                                  CIP

21	20	19	18	17	16	15	14	13	12	11	10	9	8	7	6	5	4	3	2	1
13	12	11	10	09	08	07	06	05	04	03	02	01	00	99	98	97	96			

*Dedicated to those whose stories of stress
are written in these pages.*

Acknowledgments

Before writing this book I collected stories from many people who are thriving in the midst of life's stress. I am grateful for their insights and strength of character. In addition to those who shared their stories, several have provided important encouragement and help. John Scanish, Kathy Meek, Donna MacIntosh and Lisa McMinn read earlier drafts of this book and made helpful comments. Joyce Farrell is a kind and helpful person whom I am fortunate enough to have as a literary agent. Rodney Clapp and others at InterVarsity Press have been encouraging and helpful.

There are many others to acknowledge for their ongoing influence in my life—they help me understand Christian community and the value of stress in establishing character. These include Clark and Donell Campbell, Stan and Brenna Jones and all my departmental colleagues at Wheaton College, Jim Wilhoit, Greg and Ann Skipper, Alvaro and Leslie Nieves, Gary Collins, Dan and JoLynn Graham, Lisa McMinn and my children: Danielle, Sarah and Megan. I am grateful for these people and many more, and am reminded that "iron sharpens iron, and one person sharpens the wits of another" (Proverbs 27:17).

Introduction

Humble yourselves before the Lord,
and he will exalt you.
JAMES 4:10

Stress humbles us, and grace makes us whole. Many of the greatest problems in life are experienced by those who do not let stress and grace accomplish their work. Some have never allowed stress to humble them. As they race through a life of stress management and time management, they cling tenaciously to the American ideals of self-sufficiency, individualism, ambition and accomplishment: "I'll do it my way." Others have not let grace make them whole. They live in a broken state of despair and hopelessness.

Stress has become a way of life for most of us. We spend enormous energy trying to get rid of stress. But how are we doing? Although many stress management techniques are helpful and useful, our culture is still plagued with enormous stress-related problems. Maybe our preoccupation with stress management points us in the wrong direction.

By targeting stress as the enemy, we have become less tolerant of it. We have developed a whole vocabulary of stress-related words to help us address this subject, but it seems our stress literacy has only created a preoccupation, a fantasy, about living lives free of stress. The more we focus on stress, the more we believe it is bad. Our negative attitude toward stress only strengthens its grip on our lives.

In order to be more tolerant of stress, we need to think about it differently. Stress is neither bad nor good, but it brings with it valuable opportunities for insight and growth. We become tolerant of stress only as we learn to embrace it as an inevitable and useful part of being human.

This is not a book about catastrophic pain. I am aware of the crises of life, both professionally and personally. As a psychologist, I often sit with clients who are experiencing enormous pain. I also face crises in my own life. We do no favors when we point out the lessons of pain to those who are engulfed by it. People in crisis situations are not helped by hearing that all things work together for good. Trite words of encouragement are often experienced as tiny, sticky Band-aids on gaping wounds. If you are in the midst of a catastrophe, you need to be nurtured, embraced and encouraged. You need to cry more than you need to read this book.

This book is intended to help us find value in the stress that we ourselves experience. I pray this book will be used for self-awareness and personal insight rather than as a source of insensitive advice to be passed on to hurting people. Further, I pray this book will never be used to justify oppression. Coping with our own stress is one thing. Hurting others and assuming that stress will be good for them is another. Oppression should break our hearts, whether or not there is value in stress.

This is a book about the stress we face every day—the stress resulting from the oil leak in the car, the pile of clothes needing to be ironed, the dripping faucet, the orthodontic consultation you need to arrange, the gutters that need cleaning, the report that was due yesterday and the phone calls you still need to return today. These hassles may seem worthless, but they are not. They are God's tools for shaping our character.

As I collected information for this book, I interviewed persons living with high levels of stress. They remind us all that hope comes not from the circumstances of life, but from the inner life that is nourished by our gracious God.

1

The Big Squeeze

Grandma didn't really need to warn me, but she did anyway. Whenever I came within three feet of the washtub, she cautioned me to keep my fingers away from the wringer. She didn't have to worry. My six-year-old brain had studied what the wringer did to her laundry, and making pancakes out of my fingers was low on my list of childhood entertainment options. I was more concerned for *her* fingers. They seemed to come close to demise each time she loaded her next dripping victim into those rubber jaws. I imagined watching the wringer grab and smash her fingers, her hand, her arm, her shoulder, her torso . . . You get the picture—Grandma in two dimensions.

But Grandma never got caught in her wringer. She lived out her years with Grandpa on their Oregon farm, harvesting fruit, doing laundry in that familiar basement, cooking, sewing, encouraging her children, making cookies with her grandchildren and occasionally venturing into town to buy supplies. Although she must have lived with her own pain and stress, as we all do, times seemed different back then. Those were the days before the information explosion and the electronic revolution, back when television was a new invention.

As times have changed, so have the stressors in our lives. The wringers on washing machines are gone, and modern equipment helps us save time. But where does the extra time go? With all our efficiency, we still have too much to do.

That horrible picture in my mind, of Grandma getting sucked into that wringer and coming out the other side like Sylvester the Cat on the wrong side of a steamroller, causes me to stop and reflect on life in the fast-paced information age. How often do we feel like a smashed pancake by the end of the week? How often are we so drained of energy that we have no time for the things we care about the most? How often do our spiritual lives reflect the vapid feeling inside that comes from living under daily pressure? Life in this era of overachievement and overabundance can often feel like life in the wringer.

Surrounded by Stress

Contemporary life is filled with all sorts of blessings, trials and stressors—bills, expectations, deadlines, exercise routines, church responsibilities, children, grandchildren, investments, committees and so much more. Although many of these are good opportunities, sometimes they feel overwhelming, as if we are in that wringer, being squeezed, smashed and deformed between rigid responsibilities.

Almost everyone is familiar with a life of pressure and stress. Six out of ten Americans report feeling "great stress" once a week or more.[1] We see the effects of stress depicted grotesquely on tabloid covers as we wait in line to pay for our groceries. Business executives discuss time pressures with colleagues and friends on their cellular phones while waiting in stalled traffic. We think about quick ways to prepare meals while driving children from one activity to another. We fit more into twenty-four hours by sleeping less, praying less, socializing less, drinking more coffee and doing two or three things at once.

Often we equate stress with life's catastrophes and major changes. Many have seen popularized versions of the Holmes and Rahe Social Readjustment Scale, a stress scale which assigns a certain number of points to each major life change. The total number of points equals the amount of stress in the past six months. But newer research demonstrates that the stress of life doesn't come just from major catastrophes.

Joan, a twenty-five-year-old married woman, is feeling stressed because her father died suddenly of a heart attack. Her appetite is poor, she is having nightmares about her father's death, and she cries frequently.

Barb is also twenty-five years old but has a healthy father. Her biggest worries are getting the kids to Little League practice on time, balancing the budget on a limited income and losing a few pounds before summer.

Both Joan and Barb experience stress, but who is more vulnerable to the negative effects of stress? You might be surprised to discover that Barb is likely to experience at least as many stress-related problems as Joan. Joan is experiencing the effects of catastrophic stress, but Barb is living with subtle, chronic forms of stress every day. She sees stress in street clothes— the way stress looks day in and day out.

Psychologist Richard Lazarus found that daily hassles add the greatest pressure to life.[2] Imagine each little hassle as a brick—losing your keys, taking your child to piano lessons, fixing the leaky faucet or the plugged bathroom drain, losing your keys again, dieting, paying for a home security system, misplacing your checkbook, raking autumn leaves. No one brick by itself is too heavy, but when you add up all the bricks the load can seem overwhelming. Lazarus surveyed one hundred adults and reported their ten most common hassles. Here is stress in street clothes—the top ten hassles in life.

Hassle 10: Physical Appearance

There is little doubt that physical beauty attracts attention. A study published in 1976 demonstrated that experts who give us illogical arguments will not cause us to change our attitudes, but an attractive nonexpert who gives the same argument will cause us to change.[3] Those who are attractive are more likely than unattractive persons to receive help from strangers.[4] Attractive people are even perceived to be more intelligent than those who are unattractive.[5] So it's not too surprising that we want to be attractive. But in the stress of life, attractiveness starts to slip. We feel the stress of our aging bodies as we step onto the racquetball court or crawl out of bed in the morning.

Advertisers take advantage of our concerns about physical appearance. We are told that double-edged razors give us a closer shave, liquid potions take the gray out of our hair and nighttime ointments keep our skin from wrinkling. Regarding our social life, advertisers tell us that driving a certain car, using a certain perfume or drinking a certain beer will cause us to be irresistibly attractive to young, gorgeous people.

It sounds dumb, doesn't it? But it must be working—the advertisements keep coming. And our stress levels keep climbing.

Hassle 9: Crime

According to the FBI's Uniform Crime Report, about six people out of a hundred report crimes to the police each year. Others, perhaps as many as twelve people out of a hundred, experience crimes but choose not to report them. About ten percent of crime victims experience violence in the commission of the crime.[6]

Crime adds stress to life. We lock our doors at night, buy home security systems, look over our shoulders while walking alone in the city. We avoid hitchhikers, tell our children not to talk to strangers and put a padlock on the locker during the noon workout. Each time we think about crime, we add another brick to our load.

Hassle 8: Property, Investment and Taxes

Things used to be simpler. Remember those high-school and college days when idealism flourished and other people paid taxes? Right and wrong seemed so clear. Justice mattered more than economics, equality and compassion more than retirement accounts, goodness more than greatness.

Life in the wringer has its responsibilities. We pay enough taxes that our youthful idealism starts to erode into skepticism. Instead of talking about the needs of the poor, we start talking about the inefficiency of programs for the poor. Instead of the evils of nuclear destruction, we think about the cost of one nuclear missile to taxpayers. And each year taxes seem to climb upward—property tax, income tax, sales tax, gas tax.

And then there is retirement. Colorful brochures nag at us to start an

IRA early, make good investments today in order to live comfortably tomorrow, buy low and sell high. And there's always the nagging doubt, What if I'm not investing enough? None of us wants to live out our retirement years waiting for the next Social Security check. So we trade in our idealism for a big dose of the American dream, working hard to save for the future, support our country—and collect bricks.

Hassle 7: Yard Work or Outside Home Maintenance
Mowing the lawn can be fun. Remember those spring afternoons when the thermometer is flirting with seventy degrees, the gentle wind sways the daffodils and you're enjoying the scenery behind the self-propelled lawn mower? Toro commercials are made on days like this. But then there are the other days. Like the days when tugging and tugging on that cord won't make the engine start. Or the days when the mower runs out of gas with three feet of lawn left to mow. Or the times when the dog is particularly regular and the kids whose chore it is to clean up after the dog have not done so, resulting in shoes that smell up the garage for several days after the mowing is done. Home maintenance causes stress.

Or imagine buying aluminum siding from one of those telephone sales-people who call each week. You walk in the door after signing your second mortgage to pay for your maintenance-free, never-needs-replacing-or-painting aluminum siding, settle in your easy chair, turn on the television and see an advertisement for Roger's Roofing. Oh yes, you recall, composition roofs last twenty years. Yours has been on the job for twenty-two years. So much for relaxing. At least the house won't be leaking from the sides.

Hassle 6: Misplacing or Losing Things
Once I left my checkbook register sitting on a shelf in a store. Fortunately, when my daughter and I went back to find it, it was still sitting next to the office organization supplies. But an hour later I was wandering around the house again looking for my checkbook register. Where could it be? It wasn't on any of the horizontal surfaces that I frequent. The kids hadn't taken it. It was one of the few things the dog wouldn't have been interested in eating. Where could it be?

Finally, I found it. It was under several layers of discarded cereal boxes and cellophane in the trash can. After rescuing my checkbook register from the Venture store, I seem to have tossed it in the trash can.

My wife Lisa's memory is better than mine, but she is starting to experience the same absent-mindedness syndrome. After hearing that burglars look first in the underwear drawer for jewelry, she decided to hide her string of pearls somewhere else. So she thought of a great hiding place. In fact, it was so great that the next time she wanted to wear her pearls, guess what happened? Right. It took Lisa two months to find them.

Think about this. Each time you lose your keys, you add a stress brick to your life. The same thing happens each time you take off your watch and can't find it again, or each time you look for that important paper that you put in a "safe" place.

Hassle 5: Too Many Things to Do

No, it's not just you and it's not just me. Almost everyone has too many things to do. There's dinner to prepare, a report to write, bills to pay and laundry to wash. Oh, and don't forget your child's piano lesson at 3 p.m.

Remember when computers were going to make life more efficient so that we could all work less and relax more? Somewhere the plan went wrong. We're more efficient, but what happened to the relaxing part?

Most Americans believe they would be happier with twenty percent more money. The nice thing about being short of money is that we can do something about it. So we work harder and longer to make twenty percent more (of course most Americans still want another twenty percent on top of that). But the crisis of a *time* shortage is that we can't make more. It's a zero-sum game. If I take time from one activity, I have to steal it from another. And whether we steal time from sleep or family, or just leave things undone, it adds stress to life.

Hassle 4: Home Maintenance

It's good that cooking and cleaning are not relegated to one gender anymore (though women still do much more than men, even in dual-career homes[7]). Women are free to find fulfilling careers outside the home. That's good. But now each family is doing more total work than in the "Leave It to Beaver" days of the 1950s and 1960s. There are two careers instead of one, but the laundry still needs to be washed, the meals prepared and the floors vacuumed.

Many women feel overworked and undervalued as they work outside the home and do four or five times as much domestic work as their husbands. Men feel overwhelmed as they do the same amount of career work as ever, but now find themselves pressured to do domestic chores as well. Wives and husbands find themselves spending precious time arguing about who should wash the dishes, clean the oven, fix the cars, change the light bulbs and the diapers. Home maintenance demands add even more stress.

Hassle 3: Rising Prices of Common Goods

Rising prices cause stress. Mounting expenses demand more income, and that means more work and less time. Most of us also have an emotional response to rising prices. Every time we see a price increase for a gallon of gasoline or a can of olives or a kilowatt of electricity, we feel mounting pressure.

Remember the gas shortage of the 1970s? We all complained that gas was getting so expensive that we wouldn't be able to drive anymore. But here we are in the 1990s driving as much as ever. Car manufacturers made cars more efficient, people shuffled their budgets a bit and they continued to drive. Money is only a small part of our reaction to price increases—we figure out ways to get the money. But *change* is hard to take. When we were used to paying fifty cents a gallon for gasoline, seeing the prices double and waiting in line an hour for gas seemed an overwhelming change.

Hassle 2: Health of Family Members

With age comes physical problems. Almost every adult has friends or family members who are fighting serious conditions such as cancer, heart disease or arthritis. And sometimes people we care about make choices that result in alcoholism, drug abuse or AIDS. We feel concerned for those we love, as we ought to. It is a privilege to care, but it adds stress.

Hassle 1: Concern About Weight

Concern about their weight topped the list of hassles faced by middle-aged adults. At least one quarter of Americans are obese, weighing 20 percent or more above their ideal body weight.[8] Most obese people and many of the remaining 75 percent worry about weight. Layers of fat are considered undesirable instead of attractive, as they were in centuries past (and still are in today's developing societies). So we subject ourselves to body wraps, fat-burner pills, amphetamines disguised as diet medication, high protein/low carbohydrate diets, low protein/high carbohydrate diets and diet milkshakes. New diet books sell millions of copies, weight loss clinics flourish, talk show hosts eagerly find successful dieters to promote new methods. Yet nearly everyone who loses weight on a diet gains it all back.[9]

Metabolism slows with age. This natural slowdown, combined with a high-fat diet and a sedentary lifestyle, leads to increased poundage. So as the birthdays tick by, the scales head one direction and self-image heads the other.

Even for those who don't have extra weight in the form of fat cells or large bones, the hassles of life eventually start to feel heavy. Stress often leaves us feeling tired, burned out, overwhelmed, pressured, exhausted. And we hope that someone will do something—pass a law, advocate a social change, write a self-help book—that will help us feel better. But maybe there's another way to look at stress, one that takes our eyes off stress relief and allows us to focus on some things (and someone) more important than the circumstances of life.

Sometimes Problems Are Good

By now I may have convinced you that stress and pressure are problems, but you probably don't need convincing. You wouldn't have picked up this book if you didn't already feel the toll of life's stress. But this book is not about managing stress. Good books about stress management already line bookstore shelves. This book is about finding value in stress.

Returning to my grandmother's laundry wringer, the standard approach to stress management is to instruct people to avoid the wringer. We are told to manage stress by limiting our obligations, being assertive and saying no as often as possible. But this advice isn't always practical. Sometimes we end up in the wringer despite our best efforts to avoid it. Other authors tell us to wriggle our way out of the wringer by changing jobs, going to therapy or reassessing our values. This can be good advice, but most people still find it difficult to escape the stress of life even if they follow it.

Maybe it's time for a different approach to stress. Instead of unsuccessfully trying to avoid or escape stress, maybe we need to look for value in stress. What can we learn while going through the wringer? We can spend our entire life running from what cannot be avoided, or we can stand firm and embrace learning opportunities that come only through living in the midst of stress and pressure.

At first, this may appear to be a counsel of despair—that we should just accept whatever comes our way without complaint or resistance. That's not what I'm saying. Resist excessive stress whenever possible. Escape or avoid it as often as feasible. But stress and pressure that cling to us despite our best efforts are not all bad. Along with the headaches and sleepless nights come tender gifts that allow us to deepen our self-awareness and our understanding of God and the spiritual life.

This idea is not new. James, the brother of Jesus, wrote centuries ago:

My brothers and sisters, whenever you face trials of any kind, consider it nothing but joy, because you know that the testing of your faith produces endurance; and let endurance have its full effect, so that you may be mature and complete, lacking in nothing. (James 1:2-4)

These words have been quoted so often they have become a cliché—standard spiritual jargon to help us survive difficult times. But if we look closely at the words, James is not intending his readers to just *survive* in times of stress. He is intending them to *thrive because of stress.*

Stress gives us opportunities we cannot otherwise find. As drought causes a tree's roots to go deeper, stress causes us to become people of depth and substance. Only when the pressures of life make us confront our neediness and brokenness do we look to God to meet our deepest emotional and spiritual needs.

A Road Map

You may assume that I am writing about stress because, as a psychologist, I see people's stress routinely. In a sense that is true. My understanding of stress has changed because of other people's stories. Their tears of pain and expressions of hope inspire me to better understand the costs and benefits of stress. But my motives aren't purely professional. I understand life in the midst of stress because I live there. Sometimes I let stress get the best of me, and I feel discouraged and helpless. Sometimes I work too hard, falsely assuming my ambition will put an end to stress. And sometimes I let stress do its good work as I learn more about virtuous character and meaningful relationships. As I have probed this life of stress that we all share, I have conceived a map that helps me understand the value of stress. You will see this map in various forms in the pages that follow, beginning with figure 1.

This rhythm of healing requires both stress and grace. The rhythm begins with our myths of *self-sufficiency*, the spirit of individuality that so easily shifts into rebellion. Consider Israel's King David, a man after God's own heart, a great warrior, a strong leader. "David won a name for himself" (2 Samuel 8:13). But the spring came when David stayed home from battle. Late one afternoon he spied a beautiful woman bathing nearby. A tragic sequence of adultery and murder followed.

When independence leads to rebellion, *neediness* eventually results. When the prophet Nathan helped David see his stubborn independence, he acknowledged, "I have sinned against the LORD" (2 Samuel 12:13). He later journaled his brokenness, "Indeed, I was born guilty, a sinner when my mother conceived me" (Psalm 51:5). David was describing the inbred propensity toward rebellion that afflicts us all. The death of Bathsheba's first child served as a lifelong reminder of David's wounded condition.

Of course not all brokenness comes from personal rebellion. Some results from being wounded by others and from the general pain of life. We are all sinners who have both hurt others and have been hurt by others. We grope for answers, for better understanding, for meaningful relationships, for love, joy and peace. We long for restoration. King David pleaded with God, "Restore to me the joy of your salvation, and sustain in me a willing spirit" (Psalm 51:12).

As we find loving and restored relationships, we enter into the final phase of the healing cycle—*community*. Here we are accepted, nurtured and given opportunity to reach out to one another. This is where we are truly happy. Probably most of your best memories, like mine, have to do with relationships: being profoundly aware of God's gracious presence while witnessing a sunset, strolling along an ocean beach with a spouse, vacationing with the family or chatting with friends while sitting under the stars on a summer evening.

We learn about inner character in the midst of community. How can we learn about love if we are not in a loving relationship? How can we know joy if we do not have a sense of belongingness and rootedness? How can we know true peace apart from God? The virtue we long for is found in community with others.

It's strange how much we enjoy community, yet how poorly we maintain it. When things start going well, we so easily forget our fragile, needy condition. Blind to our true, wounded condition, we let our supposed self-sufficiency get in the way. Marriages become strained, friendships wither, God seems far off. And the cycle begins again. Some say stress is the problem, that it drives a wedge between us and those we care about. I suspect the problem is our inclination toward self-sufficiency. Stress helps us understand our need for community with God and others. Stress humbles us and grace makes us whole.

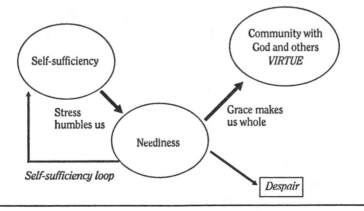

Figure 1

There are at least two ways this natural rhythm can go wrong. First, some have experienced excessive levels of stress or have poor coping resources and end up sinking into despair. The normal response to stress is community—to find someone who cares. Those who do so live longer[10] and report fewer mood-related problems than those who remain isolated.[11] But the pain has broken down this natural response in some people, who live out their days in isolation and desperation. Those living in despair need to experience meaningful relationships to be drawn back into community. This is often the role of a psychotherapist, pastor or counselor: to help a despairing person know the healing power of a close relationship.

A second way this healing rhythm can be sabotaged is what I call the self-sufficiency loop. Unfortunately, not everybody seeks loving relationships in the midst of stress. Some withdraw into greater self-sufficiency and seek relief in work, alcohol, drugs or sex. It's a cycle of damage, with self-sufficiency causing neediness, and neediness leading to greater withdrawal and self-sufficiency.

Student or Slave?

This self-sufficiency loop, as damaging as it is, has a strange appeal to many of us. We get into trouble whenever we allow stress to become master. Many of us work too hard because we are afraid to admit that we are broken and needy. We surround ourselves with the American dream of rugged individualism, convincing ourselves that we are pretty good—that our ideas are new, our work profound, our possessions important. But we are wrong. Only when we recognize our needy and broken condition can we experience God's gracious presence in our lives.

> I waited patiently for the LORD;
>> he inclined to me and heard my cry.
> He drew me up from the desolate pit,
>> out of the miry bog,
> and set my feet upon a rock,
>> making my steps secure.
> He put a new song in my mouth,
>> a song of praise to our God.

Many will see and fear,
        and put their trust in the LORD. (Psalm 40:1-3)

It's ironic to live in an age when people are trying to get rid of stress and build self-esteem. Maybe we have it all backwards. Perhaps we ought to get rid of our silly notions of needing to feel good about ourselves and accept stress as a way to build true character.

In collecting stories for this book, I discovered that many people have made sudden changes in the midst of their lives. They were once convinced that self-sufficiency and autonomy are virtuous and good. Then circumstances of life forced them to reassess. As stressful events cascaded all around them, they started looking at life differently. They became needy, and others reached out to help them. In the context of a caring community, they learned new lessons about virtue and hope for the future. They learned to be grateful students of stress, not slaves of stress.

Students of stress see life as a series of challenges and opportunities for growth. Slaves of stress run themselves ragged trying to keep up with the frantic pace, longing for the days when life will get easier.

I'm not suggesting that all stress management techniques are misguided or faulty. Many are good and useful, but when we become preoccupied with eliminating stress, we fail to find value in life's challenges. The next chapter reviews the good news and bad news about traditional approaches to stress management. Beginning in chapter three we will consider the role of stress in building the fruit of the Spirit that the apostle Paul listed in Galatians 5:22-23: love, joy, peace, patience, kindness, generosity, faithfulness, gentleness and self-control.

Awareness Exercise

Aristotle wrote, "We cannot learn without pain." On a piece of paper, list the three most painful experiences of your life. In each case, describe what you learned through the pain. Then list the three greatest stressors you are currently facing. How might each of these experiences cause you to learn?

Be careful not to glamorize the pain and the stress. Pain, in itself, is of no value. But when it causes us to deepen our understanding of God, others and ourselves, it becomes a catalyst for life-changing growth.

2

Stress Management
Good News &
Bad News

S*tress management is a popular topic. Businesses sponsor in-services* on how to manage job-related stress, churches and community organizations invite psychologists to talk about the effects of stress, news programs have special segments on controlling holiday stress, subliminal relaxation tapes are sold in supermarkets, and pizza parlors have arcadelike devices that measure our stress for a quarter.

Why are people so interested in stress management? Perhaps because stress is so pervasive. We can't get enough stress management because we can't get away from stress. It riddles us on the roads, in the grocery lines, at work, at home, as we balance the checkbook and as we plan for that relaxing vacation.

Are the stress management products working? They may be having some effect (it is difficult to know how stressed we would be as a society if we had no stress management products), but they certainly have not lived up to the promises on their book jackets.

The tension I feel in writing this book is similar to the tension I feel almost every day, living in two worlds that often seem to have different goals. One of my worlds is psychology, an academic and professional discipline with the goal of relieving human suffering. The other world, Christianity, points me toward a Christian understanding of the spiritual life. In this world human suffering is seen as a way to develop greater character and faithfulness to God. These two worlds do not seem incompatible to me, but force me to look closely at many assumptions I hold and the way I do my work as a psychologist and an educator. Perhaps you will see the same tension in this chapter. I want to do justice to the world of psychology, so I spend some pages describing the positive contribution psychology has made to understanding and managing stress. But I also want to do justice to the world of Christian spirituality, a world that forces us to look at the limitations of contemporary stress management and look for meaning in the midst of stress. This latter task requires me to be critical of the assumptions held by psychologists. I believe there is good news and bad news about stress management.

The Good News About Stress Management

Jane taps her fingers on the dashboard, wondering why whatever lane she chooses moves more slowly than the others. She remembers five years ago when her morning commute took fifteen minutes less each day. Glancing at her watch, she feels her stress levels rising.

John wants to be a patient parent, but he can't figure out what is bothering Allison. Her diaper has been changed, she was just fed, the temperature is comfortable. So why does she keep crying? He sways Allison impatiently in the swivel rocker, longing for a few hours of sleep before the big meeting at 9 a.m. He feels his stress levels rising.

We identify with Jane and John because their experiences are familiar and common. The good news about stress management is that it gives us tools to deal with these common experiences of stress.

Stress Needs to Be Managed

Two of the most robust theories about stress have been around for a long time. Both recognize the need to manage stress.

The first theory was described in 1908 and has become known as the

Yerkes-Dodson law.[1] As shown in figure 2, the Yerkes-Dodson law suggests an inverted U-shaped relationship between stress and performance. Moderate levels of stress enhance performance, but high levels of stress diminish it.

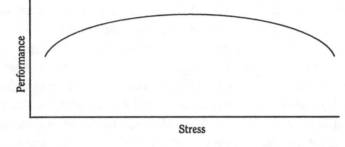

Stress

Figure 2

This can be illustrated through driving skills. Most people who have been driving for several years can get behind the wheel without feeling much stress or anxiety. In fact, we may feel so little stress that we sometimes drive inattentively. We may switch lanes without signaling or drive well over the speed limit. But what happens when we see a police car in the rearview mirror? Our stress levels rise, and our driving performance improves. We carefully check our blind spot and signal well in advance before switching lanes, monitor the speedometer closely and so on. The stress of the police presence enhances our driving performance.

But think back to those teenage years when driving wasn't so easy. Remember how difficult it was to keep track of when to push the clutch in, where third gear was, which switch controlled the signal light, how to keep one's speed up entering the freeway, and all the other things beginning drivers try to keep track of. A police officer in the rearview mirror or a driving instructor in the passenger seat raises the young driver's stress levels even higher. They may start to inhibit good driving behaviors. The sixteen-year-old may forget to check the blind spot, turn on the signal or monitor the speedometer. Because stress levels are excessively high, the teenager's driving performance suffers. It's hard for the teenager to imagine that ten years later she'll be driving seventy miles per hour on the freeway as she simultaneously eats a McChicken sandwich, puts on makeup and talks on the cellular phone without feeling any anxiety!

The Yerkes-Dodson law teaches us that we need tools to manage stress because when it gets too high, it affects our performance. While moderate levels of stress might help our performance, we don't perform well under high levels of emotional arousal, such as intense anger. Psychologist Thomas Tutko has demonstrated this in his work with athletes.[2] Despite myths about the usefulness of getting mad at one's opponents, it usually doesn't help. Most athletes perform worse than usual when they are angry because anger pushes one's emotional intensity past the optimal level of arousal.

If we apply this principle to everyday experience, we see that we need to manage stress in order to cope with the challenges of everyday life. The angry business executive will not think as clearly or speak as articulately. The overwhelmed homemaker will not function as well with domestic responsibilities. The "burned out" student will not study as efficiently. We need to manage stress to survive the demands of life.

Another theory about stress was proposed by Hans Selye in 1936.[3] Selye's theory does not compete with the Yerkes-Dodson law, but gives us a second reason why managing stress is important. Selye observed that people experiencing stress go through three predictable stages if the stress is prolonged. He called it the general adaptation syndrome.

In the first stage, alarm, we mobilize our resources and prepare to fight the stressor. As John sits with crying Allison in the swivel rocker, he remembers being awakened by her cry a few hours ago. It seemed almost a sweet cry at the time, and John offered to take his turn with her. He pulled himself out of bed, mentally rehearsed the bottle-warming routine, told himself he could be back in bed in thirty minutes and entered the nursery to save his desperate little girl. John mobilized his resources and prepared himself for the stress of midnight parenting.

In the second stage, resistance, we actively cope with the stressor. John is coping right now. He is using all the right self-talk: *I will have these opportunities to comfort Allison for only a few years of my life. I have functioned fine without much sleep in the past, and I can do it again tomorrow. I am a patient person. I can remain patient with Allison.*

John is resisting the effects of stress by using coping strategies. They are working for now.

The third stage, exhaustion, comes when the stress is prolonged and our coping resources dry up. If John were a single parent and had to deal with crying Allison every night, before long he might exhaust his coping resources and begin to deteriorate. Those who reach this final stage of the general adaptation syndrome often become physically ill, depressed and withdrawn.

We need tools to manage stress so we can resist longer and avoid reaching the exhaustion stage. If resisted long enough, many forms of stress will get better or go away on their own. Allison, for example, will begin sleeping through the night, and John will finally get some sleep. If Jane resists the stress of her freeway traffic, she will eventually get to work without reaching the exhaustion stage. Though it requires more resistance than it did five years ago when traffic was lighter, her morning commute has an ending point each day. Stress management tools can help John survive each night and Jane survive each morning until things get better.

Helpful Tools of the Trade
Both the Yerkes-Dodson law and the general adaptation syndrome suggest that stress needs to be managed. The next question is, What specific stress management tools are available and how effective are they?

Although there are hundreds of studies on various aspects of stress management, here I will focus on two tools and their effectiveness. The first tool is *cognitive restructuring,* which means changing the way we think.

Imagine being the parent of a first-year college student. She has been away from home for three months, and you haven't heard a word from her. Finally a tattered letter arrives with that familiar handwriting. You tear it open and joyously start reading. But that joy evaporates as you read. The letter describes the fire that burned down your daughter's dormitory just as she arrived, her subsequent hospitalization and her related medical problems. She goes on to describe her relationship with her new live-in boyfriend, a gas station attendant. They are expecting a baby in about seven months. Do you feel stress?

These are the highlights of a letter described by Robert Cialdini in his book *Influence*.[4] The most fascinating part of the letter is the last paragraph. The daughter, named Sharon, closes the letter by telling her parents that nothing she described is true—the hospital, the boyfriend, the pregnancy. However, she is getting failing grades in two courses, and she wants her parents to keep the "proper perspective" in reacting.

Sharon has helped her parents with cognitive restructuring. It's as if Sharon created a scale of "awfulness" from one to ten for her parents. She described what a ten would look like and then gave them the truth, which must have seemed like a one in comparison.

Cognitive restructuring is one of the basic tools of stress management. In fact, the so-called cognitive revolution has radically transformed mental health care in the past two decades. By changing the way we appraise a situation, we can change our emotional response to it.

For example, imagine two people in an endodontist's waiting room. Both are scheduled for their first root canal. One paces the floor, glances repeatedly at his watch and perspires. The other is humming and reading *Sports Illustrated*. The situation is identical for both people, but the way the situation is perceived and appraised is entirely different. One is overwhelmed with stress, while the other is not.

Fortunately, people can be taught to think in new ways, so those who are vulnerable to stress and depression can often learn to reduce their emotional turmoil by restructuring their thoughts. Hundreds of scientific studies from the past twenty years demonstrate the effectiveness of cognitive restructuring in changing unwanted emotions.[5]

A second tool for stress management is *relaxation*. Now our anxious dental patient is sitting in the endodontist's chair enduring the root canal. His body is signaling his inner experience of anxiety. His fists are clenched, his toes curled downward, his forehead contorted. His physical tenseness further elevates his stress levels.

What will happen when our patient leaves the dental office? Will he suddenly become relaxed? Probably not. On the way home, he may clench his teeth, grip the steering wheel tightly and tense his neck muscles. Most of us carry around physical tension we never think about.

Awareness Exercise

Stop reading for a moment and do a quick muscle audit. Which muscles in your body feel tense right now? Most people carry around extra tension in their jaw, neck and forehead muscles. Are there other muscles that seem tense? Take a moment and concentrate on relaxing those muscles.

People can learn the physical skill of relaxation, much as a child learns the new skill of writing in cursive. And like handwriting, relaxation becomes a natural response if a person practices the response over and over again. Dozens of scientific studies have demonstrated relaxation to be an effective tool in managing stress and anxiety.[6]

There are many different forms of relaxation, but the ones that have been researched most extensively are tense-relax relaxation and cognitive relaxation. Tense-relax procedures involve tensing one muscle group at a time (for example, clenching your hand into a fist) and then relaxing the same muscle group (letting your hand become very relaxed and comfortable). Approximately thirty minutes are required to tense and relax all the major muscle groups at first. With practice, the time required is reduced. Some busy executives have learned to sit in their office chairs and go through a complete relaxation exercise in five minutes or less. Cognitive relaxation is similar but is done without tensing muscles. Those learning cognitive relaxation concentrate on relaxing one muscle group at a time, letting the muscle become as relaxed as possible. A newer form, called stretch-based relaxation, has also been shown effective in initial research studies. Many other forms of relaxation have been proposed but do not yet have strong research support. Some of these sound quite unusual, including aromatherapy, sound therapy, acupressure and T'ai Chi Chuan.

Both cognitive restructuring and traditional relaxation procedures are effective tools for managing stress, and stress needs to be managed. But despite the benefits of stress management, there is another side that needs to be considered.

The Bad News About Stress Management

My best and most vivid childhood memories of Thanksgiving Day relate to food. I remember the olives that were big enough to fit over my fingers (under the table, of course) before I ate them. By the time I covered and uncovered my fingers a few times, I must have consumed thirty olives. The dressing was great, and I always needed seconds on the turkey—just as a matter of principle. Even vegetables tasted good on Thanksgiving. Then the pie—my mom's specialty. The choices were too difficult, so I always had a "small" piece of each kind.

Interestingly, my worst memories of Thanksgiving Day also relate to food. I remember waddling to the living-room couch after dinner and groaning in misery. Those were the days when the Alka-Seltzer commercial proclaimed, "I can't believe I ate the whole thing." I understood. Over the years I gradually learned that too much of a good thing becomes a bad thing.

Although managing stress is good, preoccupation with stress management can become bad. Our current musings on stress management have gone well beyond what can be supported in the scientific literature. The bad news about stress management is that much of what we hear and read about stress is misleading myth.

Myth: Stress Is Always Bad

Because we don't like many types of stress, it is almost natural to assume that stress is bad. So we respond as we do when we see a bad grape on our lunch plate—by throwing it away.

If we stopped people on the street and asked what they think about stress, we would probably hear responses such as these:

I know I have too much of it.

Stress is a big problem for most people. We work too hard.

Stress causes all kinds of problems for most people.

We all need to learn how to relax more.

These views are shaped by popular media presentations, many of which are inconsistent with scientific research findings. For example, we read magazine articles that make poorly supported assertions, such as "75-90% of all visits to physicians involve stress-related complaints."[7] The assumption is clear: we ought to eliminate stress so we can be healthy and enjoy life more fully. This is good advice in some situations, but there are problems with the underlying assumption.

The assumption that we ought to eliminate stress overlooks the adaptive nature of the human stress response. When we feel stress, our bodies demonstrate their sophistication and beauty. Imagine you walk into the office at 9:00 a.m. and are shocked to see a reminder on your daily calendar that a major report is due at 5:00 p.m. Oops—you forgot. You feel stressed! In fact, this may be the modern-day equivalent of coming across a hungry lion in the woods.

One possibility is to sit in your desk chair and work through some progressive relaxation exercises and cognitive restructuring so that you feel better. But this stress should not be eliminated altogether, because it will help you. Your body immediately releases three sets of hormones into your bloodstream to help you adapt to the situation. Catecholamines mobilize stored energy by converting stored fat and carbohydrates into glucose. This causes your heart to race and respiration to increase in order to make more oxygen available to your muscles. Your ancestors could have made a fast getaway from the hungry lion, while you will have the energy to pull together the report. Cortisol will cause many of the routine functions of your body—digestion, cell reproduction, tissue repair, cell growth—to slow down so all available energy can go where it is most needed. You may skip lunch without even thinking about it because your stress response is helping route energy where you need it most. Beta endorphins will reduce pain (you won't feel the headache until you get home, *after* turning in the report).

And your thinking will become narrowed. At first it may not sound good to have your thinking narrowed, but that's exactly what you would want given the gravity of the situation. Imagine how unfortunate it would be if your ancestor stood admiring some beautiful flowers while the hungry lion was bounding toward him or her. Similarly, narrowed thinking helps you focus your energies on the report you have to write.

The stress response allows us to survive the busy days at work, the crises at home, the demands of full schedules. Without the human stress response, we would not function well or survive long.

The stress response is designed to turn off when the stress has passed. Stress-related problems occur when the stress response remains on too long. Energy loss, hypertension, ulcers and other diseases can result from prolonged stress. It's not that stress is harmful; rather, prolonged stress without adequate coping is harmful.

Stress researchers distinguish between distress (stressors that are unpleasant) and eustress (stressors that are pleasant). Both types of stress trigger the same physiological changes. On the Holmes and Rahe Social Readjustment Scale, stressful items include marriage, reconciling with a marital partner, retirement, pregnancy, birth of new child, outstanding personal achievement, finishing school, vacation and Christmas.[8] These items are usually considered desirable, but they produce stress. I wonder how my children would respond if I suddenly announced:

Kids, I've been trying to find ways to reduce the stress in our family life and have done some research on the topic. I discovered that vacation and Christmas cause a lot of stress, so we are going to eliminate them. You might feel disappointed at first, but I'm sure you will live longer, richer lives because of this decision.

Some stress is pleasant and not worth eliminating.

Finally, the assumption that we ought to eliminate stress overlooks the relative ease of our position in history. For millennia humans have endured enormous levels of stress and (at least since industrialization) worked long hours under adverse conditions. Survival and advancement have required high levels of stress. And much of what we have learned about human character, fortitude, altruism and compassion have been the direct result of stressful life circumstances. What if the apostle Paul, Albert Schweitzer or Mother Teresa had decided to go on major stress-management campaigns and eliminate stress from their lives? Stress helped shape each of their missions and deepen their character.

Some types of stress ought to be eliminated, but it is a mistake to assume all stress is bad and should be eliminated.

Myth: Stress Always Causes Illness

In order to survive the arithmetical rigors of school, we learn formulas. Remember the quadratic formula? The Pythagorean theorem? Or how about the formulas that compute the area of a circle or the volume of a sphere? The nice thing about mathematical formulas is that they always work. Every time we correctly place and compute numbers in a formula, it gives us the proper answer. But the basic formula we have learned about stress and illness does not work consistently.

If we asked people to describe the effects of stress, we might get a sort of formula in response: "Stress wears you down, makes you tired and eventually makes you sick." This implies that stress is bad and ought to be avoided. In one sense this conclusion is correct. Many research studies have shown that stress contributes to fatigue and illness. But this conclusion is not correct in the same way a formula is correct, because the stress formula doesn't always work. In fact, the relationship between stress and physical illness is quite weak. One tax accountant gets migraine headaches every April, another doesn't. One air traffic controller develops severe ulcers, another enjoys excellent health. One parent survives two children in diapers without much problem, another develops a chronic respiratory infection. The stress-illness formula doesn't work consistently.

Researchers at the University of Chicago have provided an important clue about the stress-illness formula with their work on psychological "hardiness." In 1979 Dr. Suzanne Kobasa evaluated 837 executives and was able to distinguish two groups.[9] She found that one group of executives did not respond well to stress: the more stress they experienced, the more physical illness they had. But the other group remained healthy in the midst of stressful events. What was it that allowed some to be relatively unaffected by stress while others suffered negative consequences?

Kobasa found three characteristics in executives who dealt well with stress. The first was an *internal locus of control.* "Locus of control" refers to how we explain life events to ourselves. For example, imagine you have just been passed over for a job promotion. There are different ways you might explain the event to yourself and others.

☐ Option 1: I've been working here three years with only one promotion. My supervisor is too stupid to see that I do good work.

☐ Option 2: I didn't get this promotion, but if I keep working hard I will get one soon. I've been working here only three years, and I have received one promotion already.

The first option is an external attribution—looking to the behaviors or attitudes of others to explain the event. The second option is an internal attribution—looking to oneself to explain the event. Those with an internal locus of control are more resistant to stress and are generally happier and better adjusted than those with an external locus of control.

I am reminded of the apostle Paul's words to the church at Galatia: "All must test their own work; then that work, rather than their neighbor's work, will become a cause for pride. For all must carry their own loads" (Galatians 6:4-5). These words come after Paul's clear instructions to "bear one another's burdens" (v. 2). Although these two messages may appear contradictory at first, the idea is to support one another while maintaining personal responsibility. Those who resist stress best have a clear sense of responsibility.

The second characteristic of stress-resistant executives was their high level of *commitment* to the various activities in their lives. Commitment gives meaning to stress. Over the years I have known many students who survived the rigors of work and school and still found joy in life.

Paul was a journeyman pipefitter making a good income when he decided to return to school. He and his young family had to move, and Paul worked nights and weekends to survive financially. But he thrived academically. He always seemed cheerful and full of energy despite his schedule. Now Paul is working on his doctorate.

Brenda is a single mother of three children working her way through a doctoral program in psychology. She does clerical work, paper routes and other odd jobs to keep her family fed and pay the rent. Whenever I see Brenda, she is smiling and energetic. She is committed to breaking the cycle of poverty that has plagued her family.

Unlike many of her peers, Robin didn't come from a wealthy family. She worked three jobs in order to pay tuition while going to school full time. Despite her schedule, Robin's term paper or exam was always the best in the bunch.

These students were passionate about their commitment to education. They thrived in the midst of incredible stress because of their commitment.

The third characteristic that Kobasa found in stress-resistant executives was that they saw change as a *challenge*. This is not easy, because change always represents loss. Anytime we change a job, move to a new house, change a telephone number or alter a relationship, we lose something. But those who are most stress-resistant are more likely to see the adventure in change rather than the loss. Perhaps it was a stress-resistant executive who came up with U-Haul's slogan: "An Adventure in Moving."

Since Kobasa's work in 1979, many other researchers have looked at the stress-resistant, hardy personality. Although a few studies have failed to replicate Kobasa's findings, most have confirmed that hardy personalities are less prone to illness during times of stress than others.[10] There are two important implications of this work. First, it helps explain why stress and illness are only weakly related. Second, it suggests that our character, our personality, is important in determining the effects of the stress we all experience.

Stress and Character
The relationship between human character and life stress is complex, and the research on hardy personality only skims the surface. Kobasa's research teaches us that our personality characteristics shape the way we view and respond to stress. Stress is a transaction between a person's character and a set of life circumstances.

Psychologists interested in the hardy personality have studied character issues such as locus of control, commitment to life activities and viewing change as challenge. But isn't there more to mature character? Most psychologists in the days of positivism didn't study the more significant character virtues because their work would be criticized as value-laden or religiously biased. But some philosophers have boldly rekindled an interest in virtue philosophy. Plato, the ancient Greek philosopher, believed in four cardinal virtues: wisdom, justice, moderation and courage. In the Middle Ages, Thomas Aquinas related Plato's four virtues to three theological virtues: faith, hope and love. Now, many centuries later, virtue philosophy is receiving more attention.

The cover of a 1994 *Newsweek* carried the headline "Virtue: The Crusade Against America's Moral Decline."[11] An inside story reported on a *Newsweek* poll finding that 76 percent of respondents believed the United States to be in a moral and spiritual decline, and 64 percent believed that Billy Graham is a good or excellent role model for young people today. It seems people are becoming less interested in what *feels* good and more interested in what *is* good.

In his book *Back to Virtue,* Peter Kreeft suggests three reasons we must consider virtue.[12] First, we must practice virtue out of love for God. Second, living virtuously leads to what Kreeft calls "soul-health." If Kreeft is right, and I suspect he is, then the hardiest personality—the healthiest and most resistant to stress—will be found among those who live authentically and virtuously. Third, we must return to virtues because we will not survive if we do not. In our days of modern technology, automatic weapons and nuclear arms, stress and virtue are no longer personal issues. It has always been true that one person's response to stress will affect the family, the neighborhood or the community. But now one person's response might alter the course of nations or even the entire world. When one stressed, unemployed man enters a McDonald's restaurant with an automatic weapon and an overdose of anger, many lives change course. Imagine the devastating consequences if a national leader reacted to stress by resorting to nuclear attack. Without virtue, Kreeft argues, civilization cannot survive.

If virtuous character helps us respond constructively to stress, how do we develop virtuous character? Through stress. This may sound confusing and circular: we learn virtuous character through stress, and we respond better to stress if we have virtuous character. It is better to think of character and stress as inseparable. We cannot know our character unless we see ourselves in times of stress, and we cannot know stress apart from the ways we appraise and respond to stress situations (our character).

I called myself a pacifist until one night when I received a threatening call from an angry, psychotic client. How did I react to the call? I climbed up into the attic and found the antique gun my grandfather had given me. I put it under the bed and tried to get some sleep. Am I a pacifist? Apparently not, because in a time of crisis I did not respond as a pacifist. I need more character training to become a pacifist.

Think about it. Everyone wants virtue, but no one wants stress. If relatively shallow character traits, such as locus of control, affect our response to stress, doesn't it make sense that our deep character structure—our virtue—will also influence the ways we view and cope with stress? And doesn't it also follow that our response to stress, in turn, will influence our character and bring greater virtue in life? Stress and virtue go hand in hand. We can't know virtue without knowing stress, and we cannot respond well to stress without having virtue.

A fitting comparison is what biblical scholars call the hermeneutic circle. That is, readers' values and beliefs affect their interpretation of texts, even as the readers' values and beliefs are determined by the texts. The same is true with stress. Stress defines our character, and our character shapes our experiences of stress.

Awareness Exercise

Think of a wise person with virtuous character. What types of challenges and stressors helped shape this person's character? If the person is available to you, perhaps you could call or write, and ask a few questions:
1. Please describe a time in your life when you experienced high levels of stress (past or present).
2. What thoughts and feelings troubled you most during this time of heightened stress?
3. In what ways, if any, did this time of stress strengthen you as a person?
4. In what ways, if any, has life stress caused you to understand better the fruit of the Spirit described in Galatians 5 (love, joy, peace, patience, kindness, generosity, faithfulness, gentleness, self-control)?

This is a strategy I used in researching this book. After identifying several people whom I respect because of their character strengths, I asked them to respond to these questions. Their stories are sprinkled throughout the book.

If character and stress are inseparable, then we do well to study virtuous character. The more intently we study and understand virtue, the more likely we are to respond well to the presence of stress.

Where shall we turn to study virtue? First we turn to the Bible, in which followers of Christ have learned about virtue for centuries. The apostle Paul described the virtuous qualities of a Spirit-filled life in Galatians 5:22-23. The chapters that follow are organized according to the fruits of the Spirit that Paul listed.

Second, we turn to our own life experiences, especially experiences of stress, because stress provides a training ground for virtue. The following chapters are filled with exercises and anecdotes to make the principles described here practical and meaningful for everyday life.

3

Love

Breathe on me, Breath of God,
Fill me with life anew,
That I may love what Thou dost love
And do what Thou wouldst do.
EDWIN HATCH, 1886

Love. *Much has been written about it, but little is actually known* about it. Philosophers, theologians, sociologists, psychologists, literary critics, biographers and fiction writers all look at love closely and give us valuable insights, but no one has been able to leash love—to capture its essence. The authors of a popular psychology text conclude their discussion on love by stating, "A loving relationship ultimately transcends everything we know about it."[1]

At least two things about love are quite clear. First, we want and need love. Musicians know it—try working your way along the FM radio dial. Philosophers know it—Peter Kreeft refers to love as "the greatest thing in the world."[2] The Bible teaches it—the apostle Paul listed the Christian virtues, faith, hope and love, then stated that "the greatest of these is love" (1 Corinthians 13:13).

When the editors of *Life* magazine asked people to summarize the meaning of life, they found many who affirmed a need and desire for love.[3] A Soviet artist wrote, "Life means love. We are here for love. Only love is real and everything is real thanks to love." "We are here to learn to love," according to a Baptist theologian. A Lutheran theologian responded, "What is the meaning of life? Love. To love. To be loved." A Peruvian priest wrote, "The Lord told us to love each other as the Lord loved us. That is how we should proceed."

Second, it seems certain that we haven't defined or understood love in a way that helps a needy world live more caringly and wisely. Despite the attention we give love, we are not very successful at finding it and keeping it. Divorce reminds us of the ugly remains of dead love. Grudges block communication between parent and child, husband and wife, sister and brother. Nations, businesses and individuals fight for rights, work to capture new territory and sacrifice love in the midst of the battles.

Love captures our attention more than our devotion. A well-known sociologist who has studied love for two decades begins a chapter by disclosing, "I have studied love because it is my life's most difficult problem. Although I have made much progress, the 'impossible dream' of a truly fulfilling mutual love remains a goal I have yet to achieve."[4] Ten percent of those responding to one psychologist's survey reported that love has been so painful that they hope to never love again.[5]

If great scholars, passionate lovers and devoted theologians have not figured out love by now, my few pages here will certainly not be the definitive work on love. But perhaps looking at love and stress side by side will contribute to the discussion and cause us to see love from a somewhat different perspective.

Of Course Not
Throughout the next nine chapters I associate stress with specific character virtues. In this chapter I will try to convince you that stress deepens our ability to love and be loved. But let me be clear—I am not trying to challenge what we all know to be true by common sense.

Am I suggesting that major crises, such as the death of a child or a disabling accident, will always bring lovers closer together? Am I denying that the stress of infertility, abuse, rape, infidelity or poverty leads to strained relationships and divorce? Am I arguing that dual careers, busy schedules, six-hour sleep periods and long work hours help marriages become stronger? Am I saying that more stress produces more love? Of course not. Stress is not all good—it wears us down, taxes our resources, dries up our creativity, challenges our relationships.

What I am suggesting is that ordinary levels of stress can produce *character* traits that help some people understand and experience love in ways they could not have known before the stress occurred. There are three key elements to this. First, I am referring to ordinary stressors, like the daily hassles we all experience. Catastrophic stressors often rip love into shreds. If it is recovered at all, it often takes years of work.[6] Second, stress and love have no magical synergy. If stress deepens love, it is only because stress changes one's character, and love is a product of character. Third, stress produces deeper love only for some people. Stress drives other people to isolation and loneliness.

In looking at stress, we must first decide what information we are to use—the general conclusions coming from most research studies or the exceptions to those conclusions. There are dozens of scientific studies that demonstrate the damaging effects of stress, but in each of these studies are individuals who don't respond in the way we would expect. As discussed in chapter two, stress makes many people vulnerable to physical illness, but there are exceptions. Those with hardy personalities often don't get sick despite high levels of stress. In the same way, stress disrupts and sometimes destroys relationships, but there are exceptions—many relationships deepen in times of stress. When we study stress research, we often learn as much from the exceptions as from the general conclusions.

We don't learn about exceptional people by reading the latest studies about stress, but by being keen observers of those who handle stress with virtue and dignity. In my work as a clinical psychologist I have read journal articles about stress and observed hundreds of clients as they cope with life. It's hard to say which source of information is more valuable, but the hours I have spent with clients have affected my life more deeply than all the journals and books I have read. I have also learned by observing friends, interacting with students, pondering God's grace, being with my children, loving my wife Lisa and allowing her to love me through seventeen years of marriage. When I am older, I will understand much more. But for now these are my conclusions:

1. Love has more to do with character than with passion.
2. Neediness in the right amounts can help love.
3. Stress makes us aware of our neediness.

Love and Character

You're familiar with today's most prevalent view of love—the only one that can fit into thirty-second television spots (usually featured in beer, razor or car commercials). It goes something like this. You're walking along the street, concentrating on your daily to-do list or conversing with a friend. All of a sudden you look up and see the person of your dreams. The person's beauty is surpassed only by his or her longing for you. You both know in an instant that you are meant for each other.

This view of love is exaggerated and idealized, but not all wrong. Whether it is love at first sight, as the above example implies, or a profound romantic bond with a spouse, love engages our passions. From time immemorial people have been interested in the romantic, passionate love that the Greeks called *eros*. As C. S. Lewis instructs in *The Four Loves*,[7] eros is not simply an animal-like sexual desire. It can be an emotional longing for another person that brings out our most noble, altruistic traits.

Love as Virus

Though eros can be good, preoccupation with eros creates problems. Perhaps paramount among those problems is the tendency to see love as something that happens to us. We are asked to believe that love is something we catch, like a virus. I noticed the following letter in the *Chicago Sun-Times* (May 19, 1994).

Dear Zazz:

I've noticed a very pretty mail carrier whose route is near my house. Now, I find myself driving in that neighborhood just to catch a glimpse of her. How might I introduce myself?

The letter is signed "Loves a Woman in Uniform." Do you see how helpless this man feels? He noticed the mail carrier, fell in love and now "finds himself" stalking her for a glimpse. We don't see a hint of personal responsibility for his feelings and choices. Even the common term "falling in love" implies a helpless condition over which we have little or no control. Is love a virus or a virtue?

At first glance this may seem to be a poor analogy, because people want love, whereas they don't want a virus. But if we consider the long-term effects of "catching love," we might see even more pain and discomfort than the latest flu bug entails. Passion without commitment rarely produces long-term contentment.

How does "caught love" relate to stress? It appears that the more stressed and emotionally aroused we feel, the more likely we are to "catch love." A researcher, Arthur Aron, set up a fascinating experiment to demonstrate this. He had one group of men cross a dangerous, narrow 450-foot bridge that swayed in the wind over a 230-foot canyon. As each man finished crossing the bridge, he was approached by an attractive woman who asked him to complete a questionnaire. She gave him a home phone number to call if he had questions. Another group of men crossed a safe bridge before meeting the attractive woman.

Which men were more likely to call the woman at home? Four times as many men who crossed the dangerous bridge called. In the midst of their emotional arousal, they were apparently more likely to feel eros toward the attractive woman.[8]

People may be more likely to be blindsided by love in times of stress. It's the distressed counselor who is most likely to act in sexually inappropriate ways toward a client.[9] Similarly, it seems likely that the stressed business executive is more likely to "fall in love" with a coworker, and the stressed homemaker is more vulnerable to an extramarital affair than those who are less stressed.

Sadly, many try to escape stress the wrong way. They feel overworked, deprived of pleasure and tired of responsibility, so they seek pleasure in illicit love. But the very thing they use to reduce stress (passion) ends up creating enormous stress later on. The long-term result is that they end up more stressed, more unhappy, more fatigued.

When love is viewed as something that happens to us, we are left feeling helpless and out of control, and stress only makes us more vulnerable.

Rather than viewing love as something we catch, like a virus, we can view love as a reflection of our character—a virtue.

Love as Virtue

Those who have found lasting love—with God, a spouse, a friend, a child—know that love is much more than a set of emotions that one catches. Some describe love as action. Others describe it as commitment. Some say it is a way of thinking. Ultimately, all definitions contribute to our understanding but still fail to capture love. Love can't be reduced to a dictionary entry or a research hypothesis, because the capacity to love is woven into the fabric of human character and is as complex and varied as human nature itself.

The connection of love and character can be seen in the other three types of loves described by Lewis in *The Four Loves*. Affection (the Greeks called it *storgē*) is the type of comfortable love a parent feels toward a child, or a child feels toward a parent. When affection is absent, as when a parent abandons a child or a child betrays a parent, we question his or her character. Friendship (*philia* in Greek) is a love that has been known throughout history but has suffered in the two centuries since Romanticism. What has survived of friendship is a reflection of character and virtue. Nineteenth-century author William Hazlitt wrote, "To be capable of steady friendship and lasting love, are the two greatest proofs, not only of goodness of heart, but of strength of mind." Charity (the Greek word is *agapē;* the apostle Paul begins with *agapē* when describing the fruit of the Spirit in Galatians 5:22) is love revealed in the character of God, the perfect picture of love that changes lives and transforms culture. Human forms of charity are only approximations because human character is a dim reflection of God's divine nature.

Thus our experiences of affection, friendship and charity are inextricably tied to our character. Even eros, which seems to be caught, is a reflection of our character. Those who are committed to lifelong marriage train themselves to fan the flames of romantic attraction for one another while deliberately avoiding romantic encounters with others. Love, in all its forms, is a reflection of character.

If love is a virtue, a product of our character, then it can be refined and improved, just as our character can be trained and disciplined. Stress is the chisel that God uses to shape our ability to love. If you want to know about loyal, faithful love, don't ask the bride and groom at a wedding, ask them at their golden anniversary. A fifty-year period of stress has shaped their understanding of one another, their knowledge of love and their capacity to tenaciously cling to one another in the midst of life's storms. The deepest love relationships have not just survived the stress of life, they have ultimately prospered and been defined through times of stress.

Love and Neediness
Picture yourself in the following situations and guess how you might feel or react.

Situation 1: Your spouse looks longingly into your eyes, gently caresses your hand and says, "I love you."

Situation 2: Your spouse looks longingly into your eyes, gently caresses your hand and says, "I need you."

Most of us respond warmly to the first situation. We like to be loved and reminded that we are loved. But the second situation probably evokes a mixed reaction. In one sense we want to be needed, but in another we are concerned about being too close to needy people. Why do we fear being needed?

One reason we may avoid neediness is that we remember past relationships with excessively needy individuals. In the best relationships, both parties are able to give gifts of love when the other is in need. But when one person is in constant need, the relationship becomes unbalanced, draining, exhausting.

Another reason we fear being needed has to do with the psychological and sociological climate of contemporary society. We want to be independent, self-sufficient and strong. And we expect others to be the same. We avoid expressing needs and drawing close to those who are needy because to do so would violate our ideal of rugged individualism. Who says John Wayne is dead?

When I discussed love in my first book, *Your Hidden Half,* I failed to see how this American individualism had blinded me. My views were quite simplistic: there are two types of love, one based on need and one based on giving, and we ought to mature into giving-love and leave need-love behind. I was in good company by making such an assertion. Abraham Maslow, a leading humanistic psychologist, proposed something similar when he wrote that what I call giving-love reflects greater maturity than what I am calling need-love.[10] C. S. Lewis also described a temptation to present love in this simplistic way in the introduction of *The Four Loves.* He used the terms gift-love and need-love, and wrote:

> I was looking forward to writing some fairly easy panegyrics on the first sort of love and disparagements on the second. . . . Every time I have tried to think the thing out along those lines I have ended in puzzles and contradictions. The reality is more complicated than I supposed.[11]

How unrealistic it would be to assert that we should all strive toward giving-love and abandon need-love. Both are important. Need fuels love.

Think, for example, of a child's love for a parent. The child is motivated out of need—need for food, need for shelter and need for attention and affection. In a healthy parent-child relationship, the parent is motivated by giving-love and is pleased to provide food, shelter, affection and many other things. At first glance this might seem to support the idea that need-love is immature and giving-love is mature. After all, we socialize our children to grow up, give love to others and stop being needy. But let's look more closely. What happens when a child does not appear to be needy, as with autistic children who seem detached and emotionally isolated from birth? Most parents find it difficult to love such a child as intensely as they love a normal child. A parent's love thrives on a child's need. Even the caregiver is needy in this sense—the parent needs a needy child for love to blossom.

Children have an amazing capacity to love God. Their faith is simple but sincere. They know what it means to be needy and are perfectly willing to be needy before God. Adults have been taught to be independent and strong and have a more difficult time loving God. We try to play the parent role—taking care of God by doing good deeds or evangelizing the world. These are worthy goals, but when will we learn that we must be needy to understand God's love as our children do? Israel's King David knew:

But may all who seek you
  rejoice and be glad in you;
may those who love your salvation
  say continually, "Great is the LORD!"
As for me, I am poor and needy,
  but the Lord takes thought for me.
You are my help and my deliverer;
  do not delay, O my God. (Psalm 40:16-17)

As adults, we don't often seek relationships with people who are chronically needy, but neediness in proper doses can help a relationship become closer. When I pick up a friend at the airport in the middle of the night, I have met a need and we become closer friends. When I borrow a ladder from a neighbor, the same thing happens.

Sometimes we give. Sometimes we need. In most healthy adult relationships the roles change back and forth, and if the balance is right, love grows. Relationships in which both parties are needy do not work well. Neither do relationships in which both parties are afraid to be needy. Love requires both need and giving.

Awareness Exercise

Think of a strong love relationship in your life, either friendship love or romantic love. Ask yourself some questions:
1. When have I risked expressing my needs to this person? How has he/she responded?
2. When has he/she risked expressing needs? How have I responded?
3. How have these expressions of need deepened our love for one another?

Gender and Need

A men's movement is emerging over the cacophony of popular definitions of male character: beer commercials on Monday-night football, *Lethal Weapon* movies and *The Wall Street Journal*. It is emerging out of our frustration and dissatisfaction with the tough individualism we have been taught. In the preface to *Iron John*, Robert Bly writes, "By the time a man is thirty-five he knows that the images of the right man, the tough man, the true man which he received in high school do not work in life."[12]

There are two consistent themes in the men's issues literature. One is the lack of intimate friendships between men. Ask men about their close friendships and you might hear about a drinking buddy, a golfing partner or an old high-school friend who has been misplaced in the rush of life. If the man you ask is particularly forthright, he might respond, "Oh, I don't really need any friends. I have my wife and children."[13] The second theme in men's issues literature is the competitive, driven nature of most males. This conquer-the-world mentality wears us down and erodes our bodies. Increasingly, men are dying younger than women. In the 1920s women lived, on the average, one year longer than men. Now men die eight years earlier![14]

These two trends fit together like jigsaw puzzle pieces. Of course men are not good at friendship if they are intent on being competitive with one another. Love requires neediness, but competitiveness leaves no room for neediness. Let's listen in on a hypothetical conversation between two male neighbors over a back fence.

"How are you doing today, Steve?"

"Pretty good, Ted. How about you?"

"All right. It's nice to have Saturdays to unwind a bit."

"Yeah. I know what you mean. My work has been crazy."

"Mine too. I've taken on six new accounts in the past two weeks. It's good for business but tough on the private life."

"Sounds like we work at the same place. Ever since my promotion I have worked five or ten hours more each week. I'm like you—it makes me really like the weekends."

Steve and Ted go back to working in their yards. After all, they want their yards to look as nice as the others in the neighborhood. See how adept men are at packing loads of competitiveness into a few words!

While their husbands chat in the back yard, Dianne and Natalie talk as they work in their front-yard flowerbeds. Dianne, recently promoted at work, describes how unsure she is about her parenting skills. Natalie listens, empathizes with how difficult parenting is and then reassures Dianne that she is a concerned, loving parent.

Certainly these are stereotypical examples. Many men are adept at friendship, and many women are not particularly good at it. But generally women have developed better friendship skills than men because they are willing to be needy with one another. While men are sharing their latest jokes at the ballgame or competing with one another on the seventeenth fairway, women are sipping espresso at the local coffee shop, sharing their fears of inadequacy, words of encouragement and dreams for the future.

Earning Love?

Is love something we earn or something we receive and give freely? The late Hans Selye, a leading stress researcher, believed that the biblical command to "love thy neighbor as thyself" is inconsistent with science and only leads to guilt because we are inherently more inclined to love ourselves than to love others. He suggests an alternative: "Earn thy neighbor's love."[15]

As much as I appreciate Selye's contribution to understanding stress, I disagree with his prescription for love. *Earning* love is consistent with a driven, competitive approach to life that many males know well. Can we put love in a category of things to be earned, alongside promotions, money and respect?

We see a similar mentality among some religious leaders who teach that God wants winners. They believe God wants people to be healthy and wealthy, successful at everything they do. They forget that Jesus did not often focus on the winners of the world. He loved the sick and comforted the needy. The apostle Paul didn't teach that God wants winners:

Therefore, to keep me from being too elated, a thorn was given me in the flesh, a messenger of Satan to torment me, to keep me from being too elated. Three times I appealed to the Lord about this, that it would leave me, but he said to me, "My grace is sufficient for you, for power is made perfect in weakness." So I will boast all the more gladly of my weaknesses, so that the power of Christ may dwell in me. Therefore I am content with weaknesses, insults, hardships, persecutions, and calamities for the sake of Christ; for whenever I am weak, then I am strong. (2 Corinthians 12:7-10)

We cannot succeed or fail in attaining God's love, because God's love does not depend on our performance. God's love is not earned but is freely given in our time of need.

Similarly, the deepest expressions of human love cannot be earned through exceptional accomplishment or ultimate effort. Love flows naturally as one person cares for the need of another—it is nature's gift of healing. Marriages grow deeper as one partner nurtures the other through difficult life circumstances, and then the one who is nursed back to strength becomes the encourager for the other when the need arises. Friendships thrive when one friend asks another for a favor and then grants a favor back as the need arises. Need fuels love.

Stress and Neediness

If need is a catalyst for loving relationships, what helps us recognize need? Stress. I wish it were not so. I wish, for example, that I continually recognized my needy position before God so that I could cling tenaciously to God's gracious and unfailing love. I wish I could always remember how much I depend on Lisa as my lifelong partner. I wish my children would remember that they need their parents' wisdom when confronting teenage challenges. But in the midst of life's comforts, pleasures and successes, it is easy to forget neediness. Then the stress generated by our self-sufficiency knocks us back, and we remember again.

This rhythm of healing is clearly seen in developing the virtue of love (see figure 3). Stress opens our eyes to our need, and the gracious presence

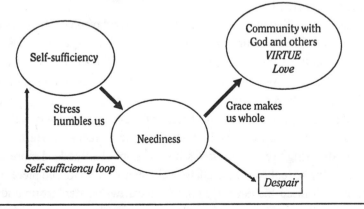

Figure 3

of others allows us to learn more about love. We learn to accept love in the midst of our need and give love to others in their need. Love is a virtue.

Love Abounding in Stress

Eleanor Roosevelt knew about stress. Her father was an alcoholic, and her mother rejected her during her adolescent years. So Eleanor went to live with her overprotective grandmother. She was a homely child who was not allowed to have playmates. She later married a lawyer, who developed polio in 1921. Eleanor supported her husband and helped him maintain his vigor. Eventually he became president of the United States. But her marriage started to crumble. In her mid-thirties Eleanor realized that her husband was being unfaithful to her. Franklin Roosevelt's mistress was his passionate love, but he remained married to Eleanor for political reasons. Sadly, their marriage was a sham maintained for political purposes.[16]

But something happened to Eleanor as she turned from her marriage toward other ways of showing love. She raised a large family, visited battlefronts, was active in civil rights and ultimately became ambassador to the United Nations. Undoubtedly stress took its toll on Eleanor Roosevelt's life, but she used her painful experiences to develop strong character. There must have been many days in her childhood and adulthood when she thought about her needy condition. This activated her to fight for others' needs. Though she lost the passionate love of her life, she showed love and empathy to others.

It would be a happier story if the Roosevelts had resolved their marriage problems before Franklin Roosevelt died in 1945. Instead, the Roosevelts' story highlights the stress of life, the pain of living in a fallen world and the possibilities of developing virtuous love in the midst of stress. Novelist Robert Louis Stevenson wrote, "Life is not a matter of holding good cards but of playing a poor hand well." Eleanor Roosevelt played very well.

I also think of a former client, an alcoholic in recovery. He may have started drinking to cope with stress, but the alcohol only added more stress. But one day he looked at himself, thought about the shattered pieces of his life and admitted his need. He joined a local twelve-step group and now sponsors others as they recover from alcoholism. Every time an alcoholic becomes sober, joins Alcoholics Anonymous as a sponsor and helps other alcoholics become sober, we see love prospering from stress.

Finally, I think of the married couples who don't fall prey to the divorce statistics. We hear about how many couples get divorced, but what about those who do not? So many have endured the trials of life—difficulties with children, career struggles, economic hardship—and remain in love. They have learned to admit needs and give support to one another. Their love reflects character that has emerged from years of stress.

Stress is with us to stay. Even in the midst of healthy loving relationships, we feel stress. The question is not how we can eliminate stress, but what we can learn from the stress we face. Stress shapes character, and character shapes love.

4

Joy

Teach us how to love each other,
Lift us to the Joy Divine.
HENRY VAN DYKE

W*hat is better than an exuberant, joyous child? OK, maybe a* napping child is better if the child is particularly exuberant and the morning particularly long, but we're usually happy when the child awakens after a long nap. A healthy child in a secure environment loves life, enjoys playing, reaches out to include others and emits almost constant sounds of jubilee. My youngest daughter was particularly exuberant as a young child and talked relentlessly. One day when she was three, she ran toward the bathroom exclaiming, "I have to hurry, my blabber is full." Lisa and I smiled at each other and nodded. But we wouldn't have wanted it any other way. Megan's exuberance has kept our home infused with energy and hope.

Do you ever wonder about what happens to all the joy that young children have? Before long they are worried about wearing the right brand of jeans or shoes, getting a stylish haircut and saving enough money for their favorite CD. They still show signs of joy, but the exuberance has died down a bit. Eventually they become adults and do adult things: pay bills, commute to work, sort odd socks and save for retirement. Their early exuberance erodes into sterile responsibility. Where did the joy go?

One person I asked about stress reported that she didn't have any words of wisdom to contribute to my book because she believes stress just wears us down until we die. In one sense she is right. We gain responsibility and lose freedom as we grow. Stress piles up like a load of heavy bricks and sometimes extracts what is left of our youthful exuberance. But this pessimistic view overlooks a different kind of joy—a less exuberant form that thrives despite difficult circumstances, motivates us and gives us hope in the midst of life's trials.

Another person I talked with had a more positive response. After living through several particularly stressful years, she concluded that we are created for joy, found most completely in the arms of God. Rather than continuing to look for joy in other people, she settled into a stable, joyful relationship with a loving God. This is a different type of joy than that expressed by an exuberant child. This mature joy is what Quincy Jones, a musician, reported when he was "blessed" with a brain aneurysm. Blessed, he says! How was he blessed? "I was given the opportunity to renew my basic belief in the importance of spirituality, reopening communications on a one-to-one basis with the Creator."[1]

Stress leads some away from joy and others toward a mature spiritual joy. What is the difference? Let's take a closer look in this chapter.

Of Course Not

Am I suggesting that stress creates joy? That having too many things to do, twenty pounds to lose and an insensitive, hard-driving boss makes us feel secure and content? Does a troubled marriage create inner joy? Do I really believe that those who feel weighed down by life's stress somehow have a lightness inside that helps them bounce through life? Of course not.

Nonetheless, being pressured and pushed from all sides can make us richer, wiser people. One woman described to me her feelings of fear as her marriage of many years crumbled and ended in divorce. She found no joy in losing her marriage, but in the aftermath she found a new source of joy as her fear was dispelled by the love and acceptance of God and a few faithful friends. The stress was bad; the resulting joy was good.

Stress does not create joy, but it prepares us to experience deep joy. In the midst of stress, some find joy and some do not. Some become hardened by life's stress. The trauma of abuse, divorce, overwork and loss ferments into bitterness, cynicism and isolation. But others have a different experience. Stress forces them beyond the quest for temporal pleasure and causes them to recognize their deep inner thirst for grace. Many have been led to the oasis of joy through the desert of stress. What is their experience? How can we learn from them?

Charting the Course

If stress is to lead us to joy, we must first have a clear idea what joy looks like. And defining joy is not easy. In *Joy in the New Testament,* William Morrice describes eleven types of joy: exultant joy, optimism, gladness, pleasure, courage, hilarity, boasting, happiness, leaping for joy, inward joy and shared joy.[2] Some of these forms of joy—optimism, gladness, pleasure, hilarity, happiness, leaping for joy—are often squashed under the burden of stress. Other forms of joy transcend life's jolts and provide a solid foundation for building virtuous character. It is this seasoned joy that can thrive in the midst of stress. But this kind of joy is not commonly known or discussed.

Sitting in church on Sunday mornings we may hear children sing, "I've got the joy, joy, joy, joy down in my heart." But what messages do we hear about joy during the rest of the week? Where do we find joy? Imagine yourself going on a search for joy. You might stroll to the nearest convenience market and buy an Almond Joy, maybe a king size if you want to maximize your joy. The candy may be delicious, but you are more likely to end up with tooth decay than true inner joy. The candy bar didn't bring joy, but maybe a Nintendo or a Super Nintendo will. After all, they both have joysticks. You might have fun playing the latest video game, but the fun ends when the power light goes off. Your search for joy continues. Maybe you could steal or rent a sports car and go for a joyride. Driving fast for joy? It probably won't work. You might conclude that joy is too much to ask for and start searching for happiness. So you check out the happy hour at the local bar or the happy meal at a fast food restaurant. Any of these may give pleasure, but pleasure goes away and the deep ache inside remains.

What Joy Is Not

It's easy to confuse joy with other feelings. In *Fruit of the Spirit,* Stephen Winward distinguishes between pleasure, happiness and joy.[3] Pleasure is short-lived and triggered by the senses. Happiness lasts longer and reflects the human personality as well as circumstances. Joy transcends circumstances and lasts even when happiness and pleasure end. I'm not sure that these feelings can be distinguished so neatly (for example, the pleasure of sex adds to joy in healthy marriages and the pleasure of an evening walk may add to overall joy in life), but Winward's general point is helpful. Joy is more stable than pleasure or happiness. Most of us want all three—pleasure as we sit down for a delicious dinner after a long day's work, happiness as we spend the evening enjoying rich family relationships or good friends, and joy as we switch off the lights at night and look forward to another day tomorrow. But under most circumstances stress does not bring us closer to pleasure or happiness—only joy.

Joy is not the absence of sadness. Many people seem to have both sadness and joy. I remembered Marie, a fourteen-year-old girl dying of a brain tumor. She was sad to miss so much of her life and sorry to leave her family feeling so despondent, but she helped me understand joy as she described her deep contentment with the years she was granted and her readiness to die. She was sad and yet filled with joy.

Neither is joy the absence of adversity and trials. Remember the apostle Paul's words to the church at Philippi, how frequently he wrote of his joy and admonished the Philippians to be joyful despite his circumstances. Paul was imprisoned and uncertain of whether he would live or die (Philippians 1:21), yet filled with joy (Philippians 1:4, 18, 25; 3:1; 4:1, 4, 10). Joy is more than the absence of sadness or adversity.

If joy is not found in the Almond Joy candy bar, the joystick, the joyride, nor in the absence of sadness and adversity, then where do we find it? How do we find this stable contentment, this foundation of well-being that nourishes us in difficult times and propels us in good times? Joy, like a duck at the shore of a pond, cannot be captured by direct pursuit. We run toward it, but it scurries away. And when we try to wrap words and precise definitions around joy, we come up empty-handed. Joy, like love, cannot be reduced to a rote formula. Joy is too big for a simple definition. Greek scholar Gerald Hawthorne puts it this way:

> Hence, for Paul, joy is more than a mood or an emotion, more than a state or a feeling, although it includes all these. Joy is rather an understanding of existence that encompasses both elation and depression. It is a world-view that is able to accept with creative submission all events that come along, both of delight and dismay. It is a perception of reality that generates hope and endurance in affliction and temptation, ease and prosperity, because joy allows one to see beyond any particular event, good or bad, to the sovereign Lord who stands above all events and ultimately has control over them. Joy, to be sure, includes within itself readiness for martyrdom, but equally the eagerness to go on living and serving, even under the most difficult of circumstances.[4]

Paul found joy, not by directly pursuing it, but by belonging to God and others in loving community. Joy was a side effect of Paul's life of service.

Joy in Belonging

We can be sad or tired or alone and be filled with joy, but we can never feel empty and isolated and still joyful. Sadness is not the best predictor of suicide—hopelessness is. Empty, desolate hopelessness produces death. Joy, even joy in the midst of aloneness, sadness and adversity, fills us with life. Joy comes when we see beyond particular events to a sovereign God. We feel joy because we *belong* to God.

Consider the exuberant child, the one whose joy has not yet been squashed by the demands of life. The two-year-old plays with glee, stacking blocks, rolling trucks around the living room, making creative and unique sounds. But every now and then the child looks around. Why? To see if the parent is still available. And what if the parent is nowhere to be found? The joy disappears and frantic feelings of detachment ensue. Joy is a natural response to feeling secure and attached to another.

As a man described his struggles caring for his recently disabled spouse, he said that this experience was one of the most significant in his life. Why? Because it taught him how much he belonged. His family became closer than ever, friends amazed him with their loyal and faithful help, and God and the community of faith sustained him. He had experienced joy before his wife's stroke, but the stress that it caused deepened his understanding of joy. This man's story, and that of many others, persuades me that belongingness paves the way to joy. Consider the evidence.

The Instinctive Search for Belongingness

We seek belongingness from the moment we are born. Psychologist John Bowlby and many others have provided convincing evidence that humans have a specific instinctual objective, called a "set goal pattern," to attach ourselves to our caregivers.[5] When the caregiver is paying attention, the three-month-old infant smiles and coos. The parent loves the smile and interacts with the infant. But when the parent leaves, the baby cries. The parent returns to comfort the crying baby. We usually think of parents training children, but this works the other way around! The child is conditioning the parent, reinforcing the parent's presence with smiles and punishing the parent's absence with cries. The child is trying to belong—to become attached to the caregiver. Children who do not successfully attach to one or both parents have "attachment disorders" and struggle with many behavioral and emotional problems as they grow.

You may be wondering how all this kid stuff relates to adult patterns of behavior. Let's listen in on a typical conversation between a husband and wife and see if we can detect any attachment behaviors occurring.

HUSBAND:	Hi, honey! How was work today?
WIFE:	Fine . . . Do you notice anything different?
HUSBAND:	Oh yeah, is that a new skirt?
WIFE:	No, I've had this for two years.
HUSBAND:	Oh, that's right. I recognize it now. Sorry.
WIFE:	I got my hair cut.
HUSBAND:	Oh, it looks good. I'm really sorry I didn't notice.

On one level this is a conversation about a haircut (sound familiar?). But on a deeper level it is a conversation about acceptance. The wife is really asking, Is he close enough to me to notice when I change my appearance? And the husband is really asking, Will you still love me even though I didn't notice? The critical variable in this conversation is acceptance, not hair.

If the same husband gets his hair cut a week later, we might observe a different conversation:

WIFE: Whoa. You really got your hair cut!

HUSBAND: It's a little more contemporary than I wanted.
                 Do you like it?

WIFE: I guess.

HUSBAND: What's that supposed to mean?

WIFE: It just takes a little getting used to.

HUSBAND: So you don't like it.

WIFE: I didn't say that.

It's not hard to figure out what she thinks about his haircut—she hates it! He does too. But again, the conversation is not about hair as much as it is about acceptance. The husband is asking, Am I still acceptable to you despite my ugly haircut? The wife is asking, Am I still acceptable to you if I tell you your haircut is ugly? Unlike infants, adults disguise their longing for acceptance. But most people continue to seek attachment throughout life.

The Search for Affiliation

Consider our natural desire to affiliate with others. Remember the first day at a new school? Which option is more likely to describe a new college student arriving on campus?

☐ *Option A:* I sure hope I excel academically here! It is really important to study hard, do my best and get good grades so I can go on to graduate school.

☐ *Option B:* I sure hope I find some friends here. I don't know anyone yet—maybe I'll meet someone at dinner tonight. When is my roommate going to show up? What if we don't get along?

Although both worries are common, I'll cast my vote for option B. Once friendships have been established, the student may start thinking about academic excellence.

Psychologist Abraham Maslow proposed a hierarchy of needs, suggesting that we consider needs for competence, achievement, independence and self-esteem only after we sense love and belongingness.[6] If we are not attached to others, belongingness becomes our first priority (assuming our physical needs and safety needs have been met). It's like an alarm system. Our emotions trigger an alarm reaction when we are not attached to anyone, and we begin seeking companionship. When we find a companion, we feel joy and the emotional alarm shuts off. We must be cautious not to apply Maslow's ideas to every situation or culture, but his general conclusions help us understand the emotional importance of belonging.

Our Deepest Joy
Identify the most joyful times in your life. Do you think of wonderful meals, loud parties or unusual personal achievements? Or do you think of times of quiet belonging—to God, a community of friends, spouse or family. Images of pleasure might include eating a decadent dessert, sinking a game-winning basket or diving into a swimming pool on a hot summer day. But images of joy are built around belonging—sitting around a crackling campfire and chatting with friends, falling in love, feeling the support of family and friends during a crisis, falling asleep in the arms of a caring spouse, strolling along the beach with a loved one, worshiping God by yourself or within a community of believers.

Awareness Exercise
Write a page about the time in life when you had the deepest joy. Focus your thoughts and words around these questions:
1. How was your joy different from pleasure you have experienced?
2. In your time of joy, to whom did you feel closest? Do you recall a sense of belongingness?
3. How did your joy help you cope with sadness and stress in your life?

Joy in Belonging to God
We may have faith in a just and merciful God, attend church, read the Bible and even teach from the pulpit, but know very little about joy. Faith that produces joy is found in belonging to God. The cognitive part of our faith is one thing—experiencing joy is another.

We experience joy when we understand that we belong to God. This joy grows as we train ourselves, through spiritual disciplines, to experience God's continual presence. It's just as the children sing: Joy is the flag flying high from the castle of our hearts because the King is in residence there.

When Cyprian, bishop of Carthage, wrote to his friend Donatus in A.D. 248, he had this to say about Christians: "I have found a quiet and holy people. They have discovered a joy which is a thousand times better than any pleasure of the sinful life. They are despised and persecuted but they care not. These people, Donatus, are Christians and I am one of them."[7]

Joy in the presence of God means we can cherish solitude. We don't need to fill our senses with other people, constant music or television and lengthy telephone conversations. We belong to God.

The Heidelberg Catechism contains the question "What is your only comfort in life and in death?" The answer is "That I am not my own, but belong—body and soul, in life and in death—to my faithful Savior Jesus Christ." Don Postema writes about belonging to God:

That means we are never isolated. We live constantly in the gracious covenantal presence of God. Now that does not solve all our problems, but it can give us a perspective on loneliness. It can help us understand that we do not have to be greedy for attention as a solution to loneliness, we do not have to cling to people for our identity. We get our identity from God.[8]

We get our deepest joy from belonging to God.

Watching for Detours

We feel joy when we belong, but not everyone follows the path from stress to community. In the hailstorms of life's stress, many retreat to despair or get stuck in the trap of self-sufficiency. Only some move forward to experience grace through the loving presence of God and others.

We must watch for the detours that lead us away from community and joy. They come from all around us—overt messages in the media, competitive words from others, models of despair and helplessness—and they come from inside. We all approach life with a set of beliefs, or *templates,* that shape our experiences and perceptions.

What Is a Template?

A template is a pattern or a gauge used to shape or construct something. Since we all shape and construct reality, we use our own templates in the process. Cognitive templates are ways of thinking that give our experience of reality a particular shape.

This may seem difficult to accept since we tend to believe that reality happens to us and does not depend on our thinking. If my house is burglarized, my stolen stereo has nothing to do with my thinking. But a closer look shows that even a stolen stereo is prone to cognitive templates. One person might reason, "Oh well, it's just a stereo. I can buy another one with the insurance settlement." This person will not fall into unreasonable depression. Another person might reason, "My stereo was my most prized possession. I can never afford another one. You can't trust anyone anymore! Life is terrible." The second person will experience depression and resentment. The two people experienced similar events, but their ways of shaping reality through thinking were different. One ended up feeling disappointed, the other depressed and bitter. As this example illustrates, the events of the world are filtered through our thinking. Our experience of reality depends as much on our thinking as it does on the events themselves.

Are Templates Good or Bad?

We all have templates. In some ways they are good. They help us make decisions more quickly, they help motivate us and they provide emotional energy for life.

But templates can be harmful when they cause us to neglect important information. Once in place, our cognitive templates become so powerful that we tend to overlook data that are inconsistent with our templates and latch on to experiences that confirm our thinking. We see things not as they are, but as we are.

For example, imagine a high-school student who believes people admire him because he is an exceptional athlete. He devotes himself to hours of practice, all the time convinced that he will be loved more if he can reach perfection. At times his template is confirmed, as when the crowd roars after a spectacular pass or a slam dunk. At other times he faces contradictory evidence: a peer acts rudely toward him or a complete stranger is kind and respectful to him. How does our athlete respond? Will he give up his silly belief and realize that his acceptability to others doesn't require him to be a star athlete? Probably not. He might become angry at the peer or privately aspire to reach even greater heights of athletic performance so that everyone will love him. The reality—that people don't always value others for their outstanding accomplishment—is unthinkable and doesn't even occur to this high-school star.

Belongingness Templates

The cognitive templates troubling most people can be grouped into three belief clusters.[9] The first cluster can be summarized: I belong if I conform to the expectations of others. People with this template are likely to feel inadequate and guilty when others do not approve of them. Because they fear disapproval in others, they watch for indications of rejection or betrayal and readily find them, even if they misperceive reality in order to find them. They tell themselves that they have let others down or that they should work harder to meet the expectations of others. They often feel weak and uninteresting, but hide those feelings because they fear rejection. Sometimes they value agreement and avoid conflict so much that they suppress their feelings and true thoughts in order to maintain attachment. They feel they can't express anger because it might drive others away. This template is the basis for dependent patterns in relationships. A dependent relationship occurs when someone puts up with inhumane or unreasonable treatment just to maintain a relationship. Such a person may feel like a ticking time bomb because of the anger and frustration produced by the other person's cruelty, but finds ways to repress the feelings and smile anyway. On a more positive note, those with conforming templates are cooperative, good team players and easy to get along with if they feel approval.

The second cluster can be summarized: I earn belongingness through unusual accomplishment. This template is rooted in the belief that one earns love through performance. Those who function with this template are often admired for getting a lot done and being responsible, but are likely to be hard-driving and competitive. Inside, they feel inadequate, unworthy, hurried and misunderstood. They place great importance on achievement, feel a need to accomplish more and become frustrated when others don't notice their accomplishments. They often feel pessimistic because they can never do as much as they believe they should. Often they feel perfection is the only acceptable standard. They are happy to give but hesitant to receive because they want to earn what they get. Unfortunately, people who are driven to achieve in order to earn love often end up neglecting those who already love them. Before long, those closest to them express frustration. The achiever then feels a need to work even harder to earn love. In this vicious cycle, the person may end up addicted to achievement while feeling unloved and pessimistic about the future.

The third cluster of beliefs can be summarized: I only know that I belong if others do what I want. Those who hinge feelings of belongingness on controlling others believe that the actions of those close to them demonstrate love or the lack of love. A husband might reason, "If my wife doesn't do the things I expect, then she doesn't love me." Those with controlling templates may be respected for their firm convictions and their willingness to stand up for their beliefs. However, they often drive others away because of their demands. Inside, they feel undervalued, displaced and angry.

Our need to belong is contaminated by our fragile templates. One person tries to belong by conforming to the expectations of others and feels joy until the expectations become overwhelming. Another tries to belong by unusual accomplishment and feels joy when the awards and accolades come. But as the fame of the moment dissipates, so does the joy. Then the drive for greater accomplishment takes over. A third person feels belonging and joy when others are kind and helpful, but that joy fades as demandingness ferments into broken relationships.

Templates and Stress

Stress shatters our templates and causes us to look to community for true belongingness. Here is a simple parable that illustrates this connection.

Trudy loved music. For her sixth birthday, her parents gave her a plastic flute which she played for hours every day. Before long, her parents stopped plugging their ears—it almost sounded like music. Many children tire of their gifts after a few days, but not Trudy. She dreamed of making beautiful music and played her flute tirelessly.

Convinced that Trudy's interest was not a passing fancy, her parents bought her a concert flute and arranged for lessons. By this time Trudy's plastic flute was worn and tattered. Black electrician's tape covered the crack caused by her brother's carelessness. The once brilliant silver paint had eroded to white plastic. The chip on the mouthpiece reminded Trudy of the family dog who liked to chew. It was time for a new flute. But Trudy was attached to her old plastic flute. Sure, she went to her lessons and learned to play the big metal monster, but at home she played plastic. As you might expect, her flute skills did not improve rapidly.

Then one day the most terrible and wonderful thing happened. Trudy had left her flute lying under a pillow on the living room couch. As Dad plopped down onto the couch, newspaper in hand, he heard a loud crack. No amount of electrician's tape or Crazy Glue could put Trudy's flute back together. She mourned her loss for a few days and then turned to her big metal flute. She learned to make beautiful music.

This parable illustrates the relationship between stress and belongingness templates. The templates are like Trudy's plastic flute. They produce an inferior sense of belonging. They cause us to believe, "I belong because . . ." (because I do what others want, because I excel, because others do what I want). They may lead us to experience temporary joy when circumstances are favorable, but they cannot produce the deepest joy. Despite the battered imperfection of these templates, people cling to them tenaciously until the stress of life shatters them beyond repair. Then we look for a deeper type of belongingness and find a richer joy. We exchange "I belong *because*" for "I belong *anyway*."

Coming Home

Jesus told a story about a young man who went searching for pleasure. He gathered his inheritance and traveled a long way to have fun. Maybe he had fun and maybe he didn't. The Bible doesn't tell us. But he ended up empty, isolated and joyless. Finally he started the long journey home, practicing his speech with each barefoot step along the way: "I'll tell Dad I was wrong, that I no longer deserve to be his son, and that I need a job. At least he'll pay me enough to eat. I sure hope he hasn't disowned me."

These thoughts are based on the premise that he belonged *because*. He belonged when he was responsible and stopped belonging when he became irresponsible. Maybe, he reasoned, he could earn his way back by working as a servant. But he underestimated his father's love. From a distance, his father saw him nervously approaching, ran to meet him, "put his arms around him and kissed him" (Luke 15:20). He was home.

I can't read the story of the prodigal son without feeling a deep emotional churning in my gut. In the instant of his father's embrace, the son's templates were shattered. He didn't belong to his father *because* of his actions or attitudes, he belonged *anyway,* despite his rebellion and selfishness.

The deepest joy comes from grace—knowing we belong anyway. After the trials of life have stripped away our formulas for belonging, there is at least one who loves us anyway. The apostle Paul writes:

> For I am convinced that neither death, nor life, nor angels, nor rulers, nor things present, nor things to come, nor powers, nor height, nor depth, nor anything else in all creation, will be able to separate us from the love of God in Christ Jesus our Lord. (Romans 8:38-39)

Those who know true joy know what it means to belong to God and to others without having to earn approval.

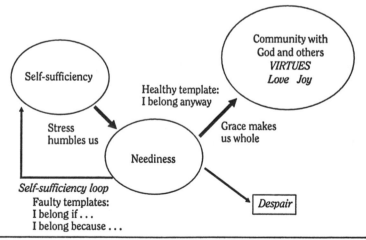

Figure 4

Does this deep joy take away pain? Of course not. When C. S. Lewis described his conversion to Christianity in *Surprised by Joy,*[10] he correctly observed that life after conversion has the same stabs of pain as life before. But he notes an important difference. Before knowing God, pain seems overwhelming. Once we belong to God, we realize that pain serves to point us toward someone greater than ourselves. We still don't like pain and stress, but they seem less important than they did before.

Stress is not good. It wears us down, tires us out and hassles us with its persistent presence. Some worsen with stress, clinging to neurotic templates to the bitter end. But stress can lead to good. Some find a mysterious joy in the midst of stress, flowing from a secure sense of belonging that no amount of pressure or tension can take away. We are created for joy, found most completely in the arms of God.

Awareness Exercise

Try an exercise Don Postema suggests in his book Space for God. *Repeat slowly to yourself, "I belong to God." Say it over and over for at least two minutes. When you are done, write a psalm describing the stress of your everyday life and what it means to belong to God.*

5

Peace

Stayed upon Jehovah, hearts are fully blest,
Finding, as he promised, perfect peace and rest.
FRANCES R. HAVERGAL

A confident rider allows the reins to rest gently between thumb and forefinger as the horse gallops along. A nervous rider hides the reins in white-knuckled fists. One has open hands, the other is grasping.

One roller-coaster patron tightly grasps the front rail, fretting and worrying about the ride. Another rider screams with joy, arms in the air, enjoying each precious second. One is grasping, the other has open hands.

Peace frees us to navigate the stressors of life with open hands. While others grasp for success and accomplishment, those who find the secret of peace enjoy the process of life and the promise of the future.

Deep inner peace can never be found in things such as material possessions, sensual experiences, great accomplishments or good friends. Just as joy and love are reflections of inner character, peace wells up on the inside as we learn about virtue. One man who found peace in the midst of incredible stress put it this way: "Before I was a consumer of fruit (such as peace and joy), now I am a producer of fruit." This man now knows what the apostle Paul described to Christians in Rome (Romans 5:3-4): that suffering requires us to endure, endurance produces character and we find hope and peace through character.

We have all known people of great peace. They seem unperturbed by the sudden turns of life. They discern what is truly important in life, and they seem to have a healing presence even if they are silent. How have they learned peace so deeply? One possibility is that their lives have been easy, that they have been sheltered from pain, and that their peace comes from avoiding the bitterness of hardship. Another possibility, one more likely, is that they have learned peace in the midst of life's hardships. Stress can help us know peace.

Of Course Not

Imagine yourself stuck on a crowded freeway during rush hour in ninety-five-degree heat with a nearly empty gas tank. Is it reasonable to assume that this stress will produce peace? Of course not. Assuming otherwise would be as inconsistent as trying to buy caffeine-free diet Jolt cola or saying "good catch" to a volleyball player.

Or imagine yourself trying to lose ten pounds. Everyone else in your family decides to make a run to the store for premium mint chocolate chip ice cream. As they walk in the back door, grocery bags in hand (no one can pick up just one thing at the grocery store), is it likely you will feel overwhelmed with peace? Of course not.

It's important to remember that something goes between stress and peace. Stress is the catalyst for deepening character and faith, and peace flows naturally from a life of virtue and devotion.

Part of the difficulty in understanding the relationship between stress and peace is that we often define peace poorly. We think of peace as the absence of conflict. If two countries aren't killing off one another's young adults, they are at peace. When harried parents finally get the children to bed, they have a few moments of peace. When two people stop fighting about past hurts, they have made peace. A group that doesn't believe in war is called peace-loving (though Woody Allen once said he was so passive that he got beaten up by Quakers). But when the apostle Paul describes peace as the fruit of God's Spirit, he is referring to something much greater than the absence of conflict. Paul's idea of peace is being in a state of inner wholeness and community with others.[1]

Peace?

Couple A lives in conflict. They fight about almost everything: who disciplines the kids, how the laundry is done, whose turn it is to cook, who spends the most money and so on.

Couple B never argues. They each know their roles and avoid rocking the boat. Sometimes they enjoy each other, but mostly they move through life steadily, ignoring their longings for intimacy.

Couple C shares an intimate love. Each has a deep longing and profound empathy for the other. Although they are apart most days, they always see themselves as a team. Sometimes they argue, but they are committed to reconciliation.

No one would suggest that Couple A knows peace. What about Couple B? Using the popular definition of peace, peace as absence of conflict, they have a peaceful marriage. But doesn't Couple C know something about peace that the others don't? Peace is not just the absence of conflict. It is a state of inner wholeness and community with others that gives contentment with yesterday, meaning for today and hope for tomorrow.

Words fail when we try to describe such peace, so I resort to an image of our hands. White-knuckled, clench-fisted grasping leads to anxiety and despair. Outstretched hands, palms open, reaching up—this is the posture for inner peace.

Grasping

Sometimes we see more envy than community, more competition than harmony, more accumulating than sharing, more concern with image than integrity. In this world of grasping for success, how can we know peace?

A number of years ago two cardiologists noticed that the office furniture in their waiting room was wearing out in an unusual way. The material on their chairs was thinning near the front of the seats rather than on the back of the seats. What made their patients sit on the edge of their chairs while in the waiting room? Maybe some behavior pattern was contributing to heart disease. This coincidental discovery by Ray Rosenman and Meyer

Friedman led to the first research on Type A personality. Type A people are competitive, on-the-go, hard-driving, perfectionistic and excessively ambitious. They try to get more and more done in less and less time.[2] Initial studies done by Friedman, Rosenman and their colleagues showed a link between Type A behavior patterns and coronary heart disease,[3] though recent research has revealed that this link is more complex than initially thought.[4]

The Type A personality has become a sort of icon for contemporary life. Though most of us don't have classic Type A behavior patterns, we can identify with the frantic pace that drives Type A people. A cartoon caption proclaims: "God put me on earth to accomplish a certain number of things. Right now I am so far behind, I will never die." There was a time when the greeting "How are you?" elicited the inevitable "I'm fine." Now we're more likely to hear something like "I'm OK. I've been busy lately, but I'm getting by." Dual careers, Little League, piano lessons, low-fat cooking and exercising all take time. As we squeeze more and more into our schedules, we begin to sit on the edge of the chair and feel the pressure that typifies the Type A style. Headaches have become a way of life for many. In one study, 53 percent of those with migraine headaches showed evidence of Type A behavior patterns.[5]

Grasping ambition has become a way of life for many. Even those who aren't Type A are familiar with the frantic feeling of having too much to do and not enough time to do it. What are we to do? Here are four options.

Option 1: Only the Strong Survive

One possible explanation is to excuse ourselves by claiming that contemporary life requires us to grasp for success in order to survive. How often do we hear messages like these?

☐ If you had to do as much as I have to do, you would be tense too!

☐ I have to keep up this pace in order to succeed.

☐ Only the strong survive.

☐ There is no such thing as a free lunch.

According to this way of thinking, high-stress lives require us to grasp one rung of the ladder after the other as we climb to success. We can't afford to stop long enough to think about peace—at least not right now. "I'll find out about peace when I retire." Unfortunately, this seldom happens. Alexander Pope, an eighteenth-century English poet, wrote: "When we are young, we are slavishly employed in procuring something whereby we may live comfortably when we grow old; and when we are old, we perceive it is too late to live as we proposed."[6]

And King Solomon wrote:

Vanity of vanities! All is vanity.

What do people gain from all the toil

at which they toil under the sun? (Ecclesiastes 1:2-3)

Awareness Exercise

1. Think of three people you know who seem to experience inner wholeness and peace with others.

2. Next, create a busyness scale. A zero on this scale is reserved for lounging on the beaches and having no responsibilities. A ten is for those who seem to be always working—dictating reports while they drive, talking on in-flight phones while they travel and mowing the lawn while they eat lunch.

3. Estimate where each of your three experts on peace would fall on the scale.

Although it won't apply in every situation, I suspect the majority of those who know the most about peace reside somewhere in the middle range of the busyness scale. They are busy enough to know stress, because character is shaped through stress. But they refuse to be captured by life's stress.

Option 2: Slow Down

Another strategy for coping with our fast-paced society is to escape. When we feel harried with life's demands, it is natural to assume peace is at the other extreme. We tell ourselves that we just need to relax and take it easy. Then we will experience peace. But things don't always work out that way.

Matt is a hard-driving, competitive grasper who longs for more peace. After working a twelve-hour day, Matt comes home complaining about the boss, angry that the children's bikes are lying on the lawn and upset because the Cubs lost another game. Lois, his wife, tries to calm things down by suggesting a family game of Pictionary. Good idea, but Matt insists that Lois is cheating and quits in the middle of the game. Later, as Matt sits in the study going over some paperwork, Lois sneaks off to bed and wonders if life will get better. As she lies in bed, she equates stress with pressure, wishing life were simpler and more relaxed. She wishes she could grab Matt by the shoulders (or the throat?) and insist, "Slow down. Enjoy some peace and quiet." When Matt comes to bed at midnight, she tells him her ideas, and after arguing about it for thirty minutes, they decide to take a family vacation next month. Surely the vacation will help Matt relax.

There are some problems with this way of thinking. First, many homes enjoy peace despite busy schedules. Even with bikes in the yard, long work hours and the Cubs losing, some families enjoy one another and have pleasant interactions in the evenings. Maybe peace doesn't always require the absence of stress. Second, what happens when Matt and Lois go on vacation? Do they find peace and quiet? Usually not. The kids are too loud in the car, the food is too expensive, and the Cubs still lose! As the station wagon pulls back into the driveway after two weeks on the road, everyone is happy to get back to the normal routine, still looking for some peace and quiet.

I don't mean to suggest that vacations aren't useful. We all need breaks to think over priorities, spend large blocks of time with those we love, enjoy solitude and relax. But peace doesn't come from vacations. Peace, like grasping, depends more on the inner life than upon external circumstances.

Option 3: Pile on the Stress

A superficial reading of this discussion might lead some to the conclusion that stress creates peace—so let's pile on the stress! Unfortunately, stress is not good, and it will never create peace. Stress only provides opportunities to test and exercise qualities of character.

Consider a man with a fear of flying. He seeks professional help and learns to think calming thoughts and remain relaxed while his therapist describes the inside of an airplane. Soon he can remain relaxed even while the therapist discusses takeoffs and landings. Perhaps he even talks with his therapist about his fears of death and questions about an afterlife. Eventually the treatment is over and he believes he is cured—his character transformed so that he can tolerate air travel. How can he know for sure?

Only by flying. His response inside an airplane will reveal the success of his transformed character. Flying has not created the changes, but it does demonstrate changes made through several months of therapy.

Similarly, stress does not create peace. Stress creates conditions which demonstrate our character. As we train ourselves to respond peacefully to life's difficulties, stress is the training ground that marks our progress.

Option 4: Loosen Your Grasp

The obvious answer to the problem of grasping ambition that pervades the Western world is to loosen our grip, to yield control of our lives to someone bigger than we, to trust. We find peace when we live with our hands open.

A popular Christian chorus uses the simile "peace like a river." Our lives, like rivers, are fast and furious at times, and calm and slow at other times. Yet both experiences can be borne with peace as God's gracious presence flows through us.

Feeling peace is part of the journey down the river, a characteristic of the spiritual quest. Those who understand this river never have to choose between stress and peace because stress and peace are not incompatible. The joy of the journey, the cool splashing water and the company of others help them thrive in the midst of turbulence and quietness.

Hands Open

Living life with open hands is not an excuse for impulsiveness, apathy or irresponsibility. It's just the opposite—a commitment to the discipline of yielding ourselves to God. It takes training and faithful practice.

We are fragile, needy, broken people, inclined toward selfishness and rebellion. But we have a gracious Redeemer who loves us anyway and is able to provide better care for us than we could ever provide for ourselves. But when times are difficult, our natural response is to grasp until we regain control of our lives or the lives of others. It takes training and discipline to fight these natural tendencies and learn the peace of yielding control to God.

Dallas Willard, in his book *The Spirit of the Disciplines,* puts it this way: We are touching upon a general principle of human life. It's true for the public speaker or the musician, the teacher or the surgeon. A successful performance at a moment of crisis rests largely and essentially upon the depths of a self wisely and rigorously prepared in the totality of its being—mind and body.[7]

Those who know peace in the midst of life's turbulence have trained themselves to know peace. Peace doesn't reflect lack of stress. Almost everyone has too much to do, and everyone eventually faces excruciating pain in life. Peace reflects character, and character is shaped through personal and spiritual disciplines.

Practicing spiritual disciplines, such as prayer, fasting and meditation, does not automatically produce peace. If we see the disciplines as an end in themselves, they can make us smug, self-righteous and self-focused. The disciplines are not meant to enhance our sense of well-being or self-discipline. They are only useful insofar as they allow us to experience and understand God. They are a mechanism by which we understand our own neediness and God's gracious provision. Spiritual disciplines free us to live life with hands open and lifted upward.

The biggest problem with grasping for success is not that people work too hard (though this can be a major problem), but that their inner experience is plagued with character problems that create hostility and tension and competitiveness. Spiritual disciplines open a door for God to transform our character. Despite what they might tell you, busy people do not have to resort to grasping, hard-driving tactics to survive. Many busy people work hard, accomplish a great deal and yet experience a tender inner peace by yielding their lives to God.

Peace with Oneself, Peace with Others

Inner peace is a wonderful goal, but we also must remember that peace is relational. I believe that even inner peace is relational. Think about it. When do we feel the greatest peace? Isn't it when the relationships in our lives are going well, when we experience community with those we love? We experience inner peace when relationships with God and others are right. The converse is also true: we live more peaceably with others when we are filled with inner peace.

We are not required to be angry and bitter with difficult people. We are not obliged to be irritated and annoyed when people are grumpy or unfair with us. The repairman doesn't show up, the receptionist is rude on the phone, the customer blames the wrong person, and we sometimes feel we must defend ourselves and show our displeasure. We read Paul's words in Romans 12:18, "If it is possible, so far as it depends on you, live peaceably with all," and focus on the middle clause. We think, *Thank goodness I don't have to be at peace with so-and-so because I have done all that I can do! It no longer depends on me.* I suspect Paul meant to emphasize the last clause, "live peaceably with all," even more than the middle clause.

Peace with others is a reflection of our capacity to let go of past offenses. In our culture of assertiveness training, boundary-setting and standing up for rights, we sometimes forget the gentle example of Jesus. He was maligned, abused, betrayed, abandoned, forgotten, ridiculed and killed, yet he endured these hardships in order to make peace with us. What if Jesus had decided to be assertive and stand up for his rights?

Most of us do not live in peace with everyone, and some situations actually are beyond our control. But even these situations can help shape our character, and a character of inner peace rather than retaliation may ultimately lead to reconciled relationships.

The relationship between stress and living peaceably with others is not a simple one. Either too little stress or too much stress potentially causes problems.

Horrific stress, such as physical or sexual abuse, can inhibit a child's capacity for establishing peace with others. Survivors of abuse sometimes resort to "splitting," a tendency to arbitrarily divide people into two groups: the good ones and the bad ones. They relate well to those they believe are good but sometimes make enemies of those they think are bad. Splitting is a survival technique learned in childhood and should not be taken as evidence of weak character or deliberate efforts to alienate others. Often survivors of childhood abuse need spiritual or psychological counseling to help restore an accurate view of others.

At the other extreme, some children have too much ease during child-hood and seem to grow up with a sense of entitlement. As adults, they have difficulty relating with others because they are more familiar with getting than giving.

In the middle of these two extremes, an optimal amount of stress can produce a capacity for empathy that promotes peaceful relationships. Stress in moderate doses produces empathy, and empathy helps make strong relationships. This will be discussed more later.

It is interesting to muse on the role of stress in revealing character. Is our true inner character clearly revealed when we are well rested, caught up at work and having harmonious interactions with others? Or is our character more clearly revealed in times of stress, when we are sleep-deprived, behind at work, struggling through difficult times in an important relationship? I believe it is the latter. Stress elicits our inner character and our capacity to relate peaceably with others. Consider two examples.

Grasping Reflects Character

Neil works as a midlevel manager at a major manufacturing company. He and his wife own a lovely home in the suburbs, and they have two teenage children. Today Neil's daughter, Nicole, has a softball game at 6:00 p.m. As you can imagine, this is a major inconvenience because Neil has to leave work at 5:30, an hour before his usual departure time. In order to get an important promotion, he has been working ten-hour days, and he fears that the softball season might hurt his chances. Deep inside, Neil feels he is not as smart as most of the people he works with, and he is sure that the only way to get this promotion is to work twice as hard as his competitors (are they competitors or colleagues?).

As Neil rushes toward the parking lot at 5:45, he shuffles through the pink phone message slips in his hand, ordering them by importance. Once on the freeway, he grasps the cellular phone and begins returning calls. He is surprised that many have already gone home for the day. And the traffic is terrible at 5:45! He can't believe how slowly people are driving. After all, if everyone just drove the speed limit (or somewhat above), there would be no need for the frustration that he is feeling!

He pulls into the Hancock Park parking lot at 6:30 and joins the game by the third inning. He spends the next four innings yelling at the umpire, who is obviously making terrible calls. Every now and then he stops chiding the umpire while he tells Nicole how she can improve her swing or how she should concentrate more while in the field.

The family drives home in two cars, but neither of the kids chooses to ride with Neil. It's OK, though, because it gives him a chance to make a few more calls.

The stress of Neil's life brings his character to the surface. It's a character that most of us don't like much. Even Neil doesn't like it. He feels like a phony, and he quietly questions his worth as a husband and father. Neil knows what you know after reading these paragraphs about him—that his inner life needs remodeling. His grasping ambition has led him to a state of brokenness.

Peace Reflects Character

Greg also works as a midlevel manager. Greg, his wife and their two children live in a home that is comfortable, though not as nice as Neil's home. Greg gets promoted just as often as Neil, though his production ratings are never as high. Greg gets promoted because he genuinely enjoys people and makes his employees happy that they work for the company. Sometimes Greg leaves early to catch his kids' activities. He enjoys the drive home, using the time to think and pray about his priorities, his relationships and his values. After the softball games, his children love to drive home with Greg and tell him about their day. Greg often feels stress, but it rarely seems to show.

Notice the relationship between inner peace and peaceful relationships in Greg's life. How do we know Greg experiences peace? By watching his relationships. His inner life is lived out in relationships with family members and others. Whereas Neil uses intensity and anger to deal with conflict, Greg has learned to defuse conflict with his gentle and humble character.

Just as grasping ambition reflects Neil's inner life, peace is a reflection of Greg's character. Greg's manner reflects virtue that matures through training and disciplining one's character. How does he do it?

The Training Course

There are at least two key elements to training ourselves for living with our hands open. First, experiencing peace in the midst of stress is more likely for those who know God's grace. Those who view God as loving and available cope better and adjust more quickly to stressful situations than those who view God as absent, distant or punishing.[8] People of every economic stratum find comfort in knowing God during both times of ease and times of stress. A Puritan adage runs: I need everything God gives me and want nothing God denies me. This is the essence of knowing peace through a deep trust in a gracious God.

The spiritual disciplines such as prayer, fasting, solitude, celebration, worship and studying Scripture can never take away pain or eliminate stress, but they give us fortitude to cope, even to thrive, in the midst of life's difficulties. They are a means of grace for broken, needy people. They allow us to know God's peace—peace that is otherwise crowded out by the clutter of life. In *Celebration of Discipline,* Richard Foster describes training in the disciplines. Inward disciplines include meditation, prayer, fasting and study. Outward disciplines include simplicity, solitude, submission and service. Corporate disciplines include confession, worship, guidance and celebration.[9]

We may feel uncomfortable talking about God's grace and training ourselves to be spiritually disciplined in the same sentence. Isn't grace freely given? Doesn't all this talk about training lead to a doctrine of salvation by works? No. The key distinction is between responding and earning. If I train myself in the spiritual disciplines because I want to earn God's approval, I will fail because God's favor is not for sale. However, if I train myself to respond faithfully to God's free gift of grace, then I learn peace in the midst of stress.

Awareness Exercise

Practice now what you would like to tell God the next time you feel overwhelmed with stress. Perhaps you can thank God for keeping you safe in the midst of life's difficulties. Consider the incredible stress Jesus must have felt as he was rejected by those he loved and then abused, ridiculed and crucified. Or maybe you would prefer to humbly beg for God's mercy and kindness. Or you might ask God to use stressful circumstances to craft your character. When excessive stress comes, you will be prepared.

Second, healthy relationships help us to experience inner peace. Isolation and stress make a lousy combination. Imagine having a terrible day at work. You notice spots on your clothes when you first arrive under the fluorescent lights of your office, your supervisor yells at you in front of coworkers, you lose an important file, you get rear-ended on the way home, and the garage door opener doesn't work. What do you want to do as you slam the front door behind you? Most of us want to unload on someone who cares for us. We tell a spouse or call a friend, because having social support helps us cope with stress.[10] Unfortunately, it is difficult to establish close, caring relationships in times of crisis. Rather, healthy relationships that were established before the crisis help us in the midst of extreme stress.

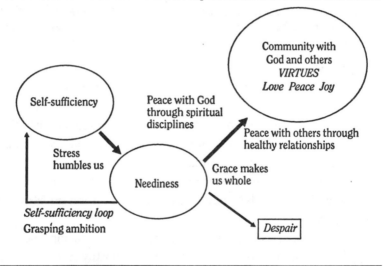

Figure 5

Psychologist James Pennebaker and his colleagues have done fascinating research on the health-promoting role of confession.[11] Those who share their pain and failures with others enjoy greater health than those who keep their painful experiences private. This is another benefit of having healthy relationships. The apostle Paul instructs, "Bear one another's burdens, and in this way you will fulfill the law of Christ" (Galatians 6:2). When we follow this advice and share our burdens with others, we are more likely to know peace in the midst of stress.

How do we train ourselves to experience healthy, peaceful relationships?

By learning empathy. The best relationships are experienced by those who have learned to feel empathy for one another, not by ease of life but through deliberate training in times of stress. These are the ones who are able to reach out for others in times of need without being demanding or manipulative. They recognize need in others and reach out with a helping hand at just the right time. They have learned their own weaknesses and so can understand the weaknesses of others.

Awareness Exercise

Next time you feel angry or resentful in a relationship, try this exercise. Think of the times in the past when you have let others down. Perhaps you have failed to live up to a promise or have taken advantage of them in some way. Perhaps you said something unkind or untrue about someone else. Maybe you considered your own needs without thinking of the effect your actions had on someone else. Think for several minutes about your faults, not your reasons to find fault. Think of your need for forgiveness, not your need to forgive. Think of your weakness, not your strength.

How has God responded to your faults and weaknesses? How then should we respond to the faults of those around us? Peace with others, as modeled by Christ, will never come by demanding what we deserve. We are fallen people, pilgrims together in a broken world, and our capacity to live in peace with one another depends on our ability to understand and empathize with one another.

Living in peace requires these two elements: experiencing God's grace through spiritual disciplines and developing empathy in order to have healthy relationships. Both are formed through training, especially training in times of stress.

Often we need stress to free us from our own arrogance. In 1992 I sat in a room in Atlanta with two thousand Christian counselors, listening to Ken Medema sing. The words he sang were familiar to me, but they pierced me as never before:

When I survey the wondrous cross,
On which the Prince of glory died,
My richest gain I count but loss,
And pour contempt on all my pride.

Forbid it, Lord, that I should boast,
Save in the death of Christ, my God;
All the vain things that charm me most,
I sacrifice them to His blood. (Isaac Watts)

I knew a lot about accomplishments, but not much about pouring contempt on my pride. Since those days in Atlanta, God has filled my life with an essential element: a great deal of stress. The stress has helped to dismantle much of my foolish pride, though I'm sure some remains. At the same time, experiencing God's grace, renewed relationships with those I love and a growing capacity for empathy has pointed me toward true hope. Though I have much yet to learn, I now know that grasping creates only an empty shell that sometimes looks like happiness but does nothing to cushion us from the stress of life. True peace, peace that abounds in stress, can never be earned.

You have put gladness in my heart
   more than when their grain and wine abound.
I will both lie down and sleep in peace;
   for you alone, O LORD, make me lie down in safety. (Psalm 4:7-8)

One young man I talked with in preparing to write this book described his bout with cancer. Although surgery was presumed successful, he wonders about the future. In the midst of his uncertainty, he has learned to experience peace. Before his malignancy he had memorized Scripture verses about peace. Now, he reports, "God has brought the fruit to bear through specific life stress."

Another man described severe chronic pain that forced early retirement from a successful career and has plagued him for many years. If given a choice, he would not have chosen his pain. He is unsure whether the stress of his physical pain has made him a stronger person, but he knows more than most about peace. He writes, "A peace that can only come from above has been present in situations when overwhelming pain was persisting for days. This peace did not necessarily reduce the pain, but it gave me the quietness to accept."

This man's spouse added, "Greater than happiness is peace: peace from abiding." These are people who have known peace in the midst of stress. How did they learn? Through stress? Without stress they might never have known the peace they describe. But their character had been trained in the years before and during their difficulties. In the same way, the Scripture that my young friend memorized during years of relative ease helped him experience peace in the midst of his darkest days of facing cancer. Remember what Dallas Willard wrote: "A successful performance at a moment of crisis rests largely and essentially upon the depths of a self wisely and rigorously prepared in the totality of its being—mind and body."

6

Patience

Be patient, therefore, beloved, until the coming of the Lord.
The farmer waits for the precious crop from the earth,
being patient with it until it receives
the early and the late rains.
You also must be patient. Strengthen your hearts,
for the coming of the Lord is near.

JAMES 5:7-8

When I perused one of the best collections of evangelical books in the world, I was amazed to find only one contemporary book on patience, a modest (47-page) study guide for small groups. I found only a few chapters about patience in other books. Why is so little being written about patience? Possibly authors don't feel qualified to discuss the topic. Patience is difficult to develop and hard to maintain in the midst of life's turbulence.

The one book I found begins with these humble words: "I am not an expert on patience; it doesn't come naturally to me. I am constantly aware that there is more to do than there is time to do it. Frequently, there is a sense of urgency that pushes me from the inside."[1]

I identify with this author. Whenever I start to think of myself as a patient person, God humbles me with a plumbing problem. Sometime in the past I learned that plumbers charge too much, so I opt to spend huge amounts of time and (ultimately) much more money to do it myself. Even a simple matter of changing a washer has never been a simple matter for me. Last time it required an evening's work, numerous trips to the plumbing store and replacing several major parts (including the entire faucet). As I left the plumbing store for the third time that day, the clerk handed me my bag and said, "Have a nice day." Outwardly I smiled, but inwardly I screamed, *How can I have a nice day? I am plumbing!*

Maybe there aren't many books on patience because we authors tend to be task-oriented and don't know too much about patience. Another possibility is that our society doesn't want to hear about patience, so there is no market for books on the topic. We want everything fast. We love fast food and express banking, rapid transit and speed dialing. Remember how fast microwave ovens seemed when they were first available? Now three minutes is a long time to wait for popcorn, and five minutes for a baked potato seems like forever. Remember being amazed at the speed of air travel? Now we complain about how long it takes to fly across the country or around the world. O. J. Simpson books were on the shelf within a few weeks of his arrest, as a country craved immediate information and watched legal proceedings on live television. We call U.S. mail "snail mail" because e-mail is virtually instantaneous. Millions of young people know about carbon copies (because of the "cc:" on their e-mail screens), but they have never seen a sheet of carbon paper and know nothing about the patience required to correct typing errors with a razor blade. And let's be honest: how many of us really read through the entire instructions before starting to assemble the new bicycle, baby crib or barbecue? It takes too long!

Sometimes it seems as if we're all participating in an instant society: "Just add water." Patience isn't our strongest virtue.

Of Course Not

There is no simple connection between stress and patience. Does the pile of bills on the desk, the stack of phone calls to return, the snow to shovel, the unexpected findings on a physical exam automatically make us more patient than we would otherwise be? Of course not.

Being on a middle-school football team doesn't automatically make one a good football player, but it provides opportunity for practice, and practice is what produces future NFL players. Similarly, stress doesn't necessarily make us patient, but it does provide opportunities to learn and practice patience, to develop character qualities that allow us to look beyond immediate circumstances and see hope.

Learning Patience

There are at least two roads that lead to patience. The first is through pain: sometimes we learn to be patient by being punished for our impatience.

While attending a workshop in San Diego, I went outside during a break to enjoy the seventy-degree February weather. As I rested on a bench overlooking a lovely harbor, I began noticing a young child, probably three years old, playing in a nearby playground. He tenuously navigated the ladder on a large metal slide. When he reached the top, his mother started breathing again. He sat atop his playground mountain, king for a moment, with a broad smile on his face. As he reached the bottom of the slide, a helpless victim of momentum, he saw a puddle that could not be avoided. His charming smile turned to panic. He tried to stop, but by the time he did, he was sitting in the midst of the puddle. He stood up quickly, face wrinkled, and waddled like a cowboy in chaps, announcing to the world, "Me got wet, me got wet."

I suspect that little boy checked out the bottom of the next slide before leaving the top. He probably learned faster than I do with my plumbing projects.

How often do we let the momentum of life, the rush of the moment, carry us into problems that could have been anticipated if we had taken a moment to consider the consequences? How often do we later wish that we had slowed down while we still could? The consequences of our stressful lives sometimes teach us to be more patient next time.

Although we can all be grateful for this type of learning, for the patience that results from the wet pants of life, there is a better route to patience. It is a consistent, faithful patience that flows from the inner life with wise contemplation and deliberate reflection. King David described this patience when he wrote, "Be still before the LORD, and wait patiently for him" (Psalm 37:7). Stephen Winward calls patience the ability to be "long-minded," not captured quickly by anger or the frantic pace of life. This type of patience helps us resist the effects of daily hassles and avoid the painful effects of impulsive choices. It doesn't call us out of stress, but often requires us to walk obediently into the midst of stressful circumstances.

A couple Lisa and I know made a choice to adopt five children, all of whom had been badly abused in their early years of life. The toll on this couple's personal and family life was enormous, but they walked patiently through those parenting years, reminding themselves that God did not call them to be successful, only faithful. Faithfulness does not stand alone—it stands beside longsuffering. The long patience this couple had allowed them to keep saying yes when children with special needs were brought to them. It took them into the midst of stress where they lived out their Christian values in ways most of us can barely imagine. This long patience is a reflection of character, enabling us to endure hardship, resist anger and negativity and see hope beyond immediate circumstances.

If at First You Don't Succeed . . .

Try, try again! Whoever invented this motto probably understood the value of long patience. The widespread popularity of the movie *Forrest Gump* suggests we still admire this type of tenacity. But there are competing human tendencies that work against long patience. Consider a few. If at first you don't succeed . . .

Quit. One human tendency—to quit in the midst of adversity—has been labeled "learned helplessness" by psychologist Martin Seligman.[2] Hundreds of studies with animals and humans show that when we cannot control a bad situation with our efforts, we resign ourselves to the situation and begin experiencing motivational, emotional and thinking problems.

For example, let's consider the dieter's dilemma. Norma wants to lose fifty pounds, so she buys a diet book at the local bookstore and immediately starts her low-carbohydrate, high-protein diet. The first several days are encouraging. She loses a pound a day for almost a week. But her metabolism starts to slow as her body adjusts to her starvation lifestyle. After several weeks, she has lost ten pounds and decides she has had enough dieting. So she does what most of us would do—goes out for pizza! Four pieces of pizza and a frozen yogurt later, Norma is officially off her diet. But her metabolism doesn't know it yet. When Norma goes back to her old eating habits, her body will regain the weight. A week later she is back where she started, but feeling more helpless than before. Over time she will start to show the effects of helplessness. She will stop trying to lose weight, she may become critical of herself or others, and she is likely to feel discouraged or depressed.

Helplessness impedes our ability to think clearly. One bright student of mine felt particularly helpless in my statistics class. As he was leaving his home for class on the day of the first exam, he grabbed the TV remote rather than his pocket calculator. Obviously, the remote didn't help him much on the exam. Was it just an accident? I doubt it. I think his feelings of helplessness prevented him from thinking clearly.

If at first you don't succeed . . . quit. None of us like to think of ourselves in these terms, but quitting is a normal human response to prolonged failure.

What is Norma to do? Before answering this, let's consider some other normal responses to failure. If at first you don't succeed . . .

Get very angry. You may know this response, at least if you are as inept at something as I am at plumbing. When the old corroded pipe won't loosen or the new connection won't stop leaking, I sometimes get angry. It's not a reasonable reaction. Getting mad has never made me a better plumber. Hitting a pipe with a pipe wrench has never helped. It's a silly response. But there is a great deal about fallen human nature that is silly.

We can become angry over losing a game of Monopoly or getting stuck in a grocery store line. The pressures of life add up, and sometimes a little event pushes us over the edge—landing on Park Place when it has three houses on it or standing in the express checkout line behind someone who has twenty grocery items when eight is the maximum allowable for that lane.

It happens on the basketball court too. A group of middle-aged men get together to "have fun" and get some exercise. Each hopes that he will be on the "shirts" team and not the "skins" in order to conceal the layers of flab that proliferate with each passing year. As the game goes on, each man realizes that he's not as gifted as he once was. The court seems longer than ever, the jump shots don't fall as they used to, and even layups are a challenge. The only thing that hasn't changed is the competitiveness! Often the time of fellowship turns into a smorgasbord of anger. And anger doesn't even help us play better![3]

Although anger may be a normal human response to failure, it is also damaging. After reviewing the literature on Type A behavior patterns, psychologist David Myers describes anger as the "toxic core" of Type A behavior.[4] Some human tendencies, like anger in the midst of failure, remind us of our fallenness and our need for patience.

There is one more evidence of our fallenness that must be considered here. If at first you don't succeed . . .

Become a victim. "How can I possibly succeed when I am a victim of past circumstances?" I have labeled this kind of thinking "the plan." Many clients come for therapy with the plan firmly in mind. It goes like this: People have hurt me so badly that I may never recover. I've spent my whole life trying to please others and live up to their expectations. Now I realize that I must learn to watch out for myself, take care of my own needs and become healthy.

In one sense, the plan is correct. We all have been hurt by life, and some have been hurt in extreme ways that the rest of us can barely imagine. The trauma of childhood abuse can linger for years and often requires enormous energy to come to a point of resolution and peace. And the evils of racism, sexism and ageism persist, despite most people's reflexive claim, "I'm not prejudiced!" Many people have been victims.

But the plan comes with extra baggage. For example, those who see themselves as victims often neglect or forget how much *they* have hurt others. In a fallen world, we all have been offended, and we all have offended. Where would we be without a gracious God who has forgiven each of us so much? Out of our own brokenness and awareness of our wrongdoing, and out of grateful recognition of how much we have been forgiven, we can learn to forgive others and move ahead with life.

The victim role can also bring stifling passivity: *You can't expect anything from me—I am wounded.* There is no patience here, only a rationale for helplessness. Consider one taxi driver's response to the question, What is the meaning of life?

We're here to die, just live and die. I live driving a cab. I do some fishing, take my girl out, pay taxes, do a little reading, then get ready to drop dead. You've got to be strong about it. Life is a big fake. Nobody gives a damn. You're rich or you're poor. You're here, you're gone. You're like the wind. After you're gone, other people will come. It's too late to make it better. Everyone's fed up, can't believe in nothing no more. People have no pride. People have no fear. People aren't scared. People only care about one thing and that's money. We're gonna destroy ourselves, nothing we can do about it. The only cure for the world's illness is nuclear war—wipe everything out and start over. We've become like a cornered animal, fighting for survival. Life is nothing.[5]

Stress has worn this man down. Can you feel his pain as you read these words? He has allowed his pain to push him into the world of helpless cynicism. There must be more to life than he can see through his clouded lenses of pain.

Redefining Success

With all these human tendencies working against us, how can we try, try again in the midst of failure? How can we learn long, deliberate patience while our fallen human minds and bodies are pushing us toward passive resignation, anger and cynicism?

Awareness Exercise

The way we think about a problem can determine the solution we find. Think of a brief response to the question posed in the previous paragraph: How can I learn patience, given my human tendencies toward quitting, anger and victimization?

Now try responding to the same question, posed in a slightly different form: How else can I learn patience, except by confronting and resisting my natural human tendencies? It's basically the same question, but is stated in slightly different terms.

Remember, one of the characteristics of stress-resistant people is that they see challenges where others see hopelessness. Even learning patience can be viewed as a challenge.

Just as redefining a question can change the way we view it, redefining our views of success can help us learn patience.

More Realistic Goals

Remember Norma? She wants to lose fifty pounds but feels frustrated and hopeless because her body won't cooperate. Maybe part of the problem is how she defines success. To her, success may be looking like the fashion models displayed on the covers of fashion magazines. How essential is that goal? How realistic is it? When Norma learns that being up to 20 percent over her ideal weight poses no health threat,[6] she redefines her goal to lose twenty pounds. Now she may press on realistically toward her goal. She will face some of the same difficulties as when she tried to lose fifty pounds, but her goals will be more realistic so her patience reservoir won't be depleted as quickly.[7]

Advising Norma to set more realistic goals for herself is helpful, but sometimes goals that point in a different direction are even more helpful. Norma wants to take a huge step (fifty pounds' worth) in one direction. Encouraging her to take a smaller step in that direction might be useful, but it might be even more useful for her to focus on her inner person rather than her appearance. Perhaps she could work toward greater self-acceptance, patience and peace with herself rather than feeling a need to conform to the standards of physical beauty imposed by a sexually obsessed society.

We often feel overwhelmed by stress when we unquestioningly accept standards or goals that point us toward frantic activity. The Type A businessperson has to sell more units than last month, make more money than last quarter, invest more in retirement, get the big promotion. This person doesn't need more realistic versions of these goals as much as different goals that point in a new direction. Why do we define success in such a limited way, closing off the possibilities of a much richer success?

Our friends who adopted troubled children had to learn to redefine success. They learned to look for success in the small victories and give up unrealistic goals of completely overcoming the damage their children faced in early childhood years. They have learned more about patience, and less about successful parenting, than they planned.

Finding Value in the Wilderness

We struggle with our human reactions to stress—wanting to quit, getting angry, complaining—because of our clouded views of success. The prophet Isaiah challenged the nation of Israel to think about their definition of success:

Thus says the LORD,
> your Redeemer, the Holy One of Israel:

I am the LORD your God,
> who teaches you for your own good,
> who leads you in the way you should go.

O that you had paid attention to my commandments!
> Then your prosperity would have been like a river,
> and your success like the waves of the sea. (Isaiah 48:17-18)

Israel had been led out of slavery in Egypt many years earlier. The exodus was then, and remains today, the central theme of Jewish worship: God delivered them from oppression and made them a great nation. But their deliverance was plagued by human fallenness. As they wandered around in the wilderness, they became angry with God, complained bitterly and expressed a desire to quit and go back to Egypt. God was teaching them faithfulness, patience and obedience, but they wanted a different type of success.

Eventually they experienced success. Israel became a powerful nation and began oppressing other people. In response to this, the prophets cried out: "How can you worship God, who brought you out of oppression in Egypt, and then oppress other people?" The prophet Micah proclaimed: "He has told you, O mortal, what is good; and what does the LORD require of you but to do justice, and to love kindness, and to walk humbly with your God?" (Micah 6:8).

Before we become too indignant with Israel, we ought to personalize this a bit. What do we do when we're in the wilderness? Do we look back and reflect gratefully on God's gracious presence and provision in our lives? Or do we give in to our human tendencies and grumble, become angry and think about quitting? We get frustrated and angry with the wilderness because it is keeping us from our goals of success, happiness and togetherness. But maybe our goals are not God's goals for us. Maybe the wilderness is not some huge obstacle to success. Maybe the wilderness defines success.

Perhaps success is patience more than wealth, faithfulness more than prestige, obedience more than reputation.

Stress and trials reduce our accomplishments to dust and drive us to life's wilderness, where we can learn what really matters. This theme emerged in most of the interviews I did for this book. Time and time again I heard words such as these: "I would never choose to go through this again. But I have learned patience as never before." Where else can we learn patience but in the wilderness?

Putting Pain in Perspective

We must be careful not to glamorize pain. Stress and the pain it produces are not inherently good. But the opposite extreme is no better. When we view pain and stress as inherently bad, we short-circuit the process of growth. As physician Paul Brand comments in his book *Pain: The Gift Nobody Wants,* "We silence pain when we should be straining our ears to hear it."[8]

Great Olympic athletes must learn to practice and compete under adverse circumstances—when it's too cold or too hot, when their enthusiasm wanes. This determination is what makes them great. They win medals because they have pushed past adversity. So it is with pain and patience. We can learn a bit about patience through reading, contemplation and conversation. But we actually train ourselves to be patient in times of adversity, stress and pain. There is no other way.

One summer afternoon when my youngest daughter was six years old, our family went to a nearby state park for the afternoon. For some reason we started having contests in a large, grassy field. All five of us lay down on our backs and had a leg-lifting contest. The rules were simple: hold your feet six inches in the air, without bending your knees, and see who can hold it the longest. Megan, who has a dramatic streak, repeatedly yelled "Help!" as loudly as she could throughout the contest. People nearby knew about the McMinns' contest that afternoon. But the surprising thing was that Megan, the youngest in our family, won the contest. Twice!

Amazed at her stamina, I asked, "Megan, how did you hold your legs up so long?"

She replied, "It was easy once I figured out it was OK to hurt."

Various gifts and talents are represented in our family, but Megan has always had more patience than the rest of us. And on that sunny Oregon afternoon she told us why. Patience isn't so tough once we figure out it's OK to hurt.

The people I interviewed for this book have been through many difficult circumstances. They aren't grateful for the circumstances, but many learned they can survive more trials than they thought possible. They have learned patience the hard way, which is also the only way. They have figured out it's OK to hurt. One person put it this way: "God's care and protection and unconditional love have become the bedrock of my faith. He does not promise no pain but does promise his power and presence. Mostly I have learned to feel my feelings and to seek understanding of my fears."

Would she go through the same circumstances again, given a choice? Of course not. But how often are we given a choice? Much of life's stress can't be reduced to stress management tactics. It comes without invitation, often when we expect it least. Once we pull ourselves to our feet, we sometimes find we survived more than we thought possible, and we learned about virtue and God's restoring grace in the process.

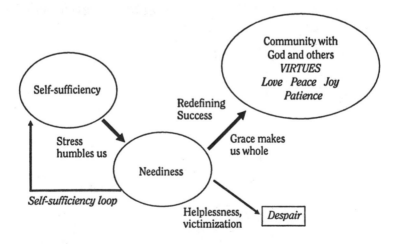

Figure 6

97

Beyond Self

These words, "God's care and protection and unconditional love have become the bedrock of my faith," play an essential role in developing patience. So much of our lives we look only at ourselves. In times of stress we have to start looking elsewhere, getting beyond our own resources and strength and relying on someone stronger. The apostle Peter writes:

> And all of you must clothe yourselves with humility in your dealings with one another, for "God opposes the proud, but gives grace to the humble." Humble yourselves therefore under the mighty hand of God, so that he may exalt you in due time. Cast all your anxiety on him, because he cares for you. (1 Peter 5:5-7)

Patience isn't accomplished by looking at ourselves and our experiences more intently. Rather, we learn patience by turning our eyes away from ourselves and gazing upon our gracious God. C. S. Lewis captured this notion well in *The Lion, the Witch and the Wardrobe* as Aslan was sacrificing himself for Edmund.

> "You have a traitor there, Aslan," said the Witch. Of course everyone present knew that she meant Edmund. But Edmund had got past thinking about himself after all he'd been through and after the talk he'd had that morning [with Aslan]. He just went on looking at Aslan. It didn't seem to matter what the Witch said.[9]

7

Kindness

And be kind to one another, tenderhearted.
EPHESIANS 4:32

T*hroughout my years of teaching, I have abused the plant kingdom* by neglect. I want a plant in my office—it seems to bring a breath of life to an otherwise sterile environment of academe. But I forget to take care of my plants. And without water, sunlight, good soil and occasional feeding, plants do not survive. I'm an expert on this.

Just down the hall from my office is a plant that enjoys the good life. It receives good soil, quarterly fertilization, regular sunlight and water.

This plant has become a metaphor of the inner life that is nourished by God's grace. When we neglect our spiritual selves, we become dry and brittle, like my neglected plants. In the midst of God's nourishing light and the love of others, we flourish and grow and remain tender, even in the midst of stress. One of the visible fruits of a well-nourished inner life is kindness.

Kindness does not come from stress any more than hope is generated by pain. Rather, moments of kindness emerge from stress, just as rays of hope shine through pain. These moments of kindness come from being bathed with God's light and rooted in a community of faith (Colossians 2:7).

Mennonite pastor John Drescher writes: "Kindness is that spiritual grace which flows from spiritual strength and stature."[1] Kindness can never come from the brittle, dry life of ambition and accomplishment, and it cannot be put on as an attractive garment. It flows naturally from a life that is regularly nourished and immersed in God's grace. In fact, for many years kindness was seen as synonymous with Christianity. People would refer to a kind person as "a good Christian woman" or a "good Christian man."[2] Even the words were confused at times. The original Greek word for kindness is *chrestos,* and the word for Christ is *Christos.*[3]

Perhaps we Christians need to pray less for success and more for the tender virtues that distinguished the saints of the past. No, kindness doesn't naturally come from stress, but kindness can abound, even in times of stress.

Of Course Not

It would be silly to suggest that stress automatically makes us kinder people. For most of us, it seems to have the opposite effect. Let's test this out.

As Bill pulls in the driveway after a long and hectic day at the office, he remembers that it is his night to cook—and he hates cooking (the rest of the family isn't thrilled with his cooking either). He tries the garage door opener, but the 9-volt battery has expired again. As he mutters to himself, he trudges around the side of the house and knocks on the back door. Bill opens the door and finds kids' things, like *The Cat in the Hat* without the last few pages, everywhere.

Rich is coming home early after a light day at work. The garage door opens perfectly, and he walks in the house to the smell of lasagna baking (his favorite aroma!). As he looks around, he sees kids' things everywhere.

Which parent is most likely to demonstrate kindness? My vote goes to Rich. When we're sleep-deprived or physically ill or overworked, most of us feel tense and irritable. Bill will probably behave irritably. Rich may not.

Does stress directly create kindness? Of course not. Nonetheless, stress prepares us to recognize moments of kindness and to develop character traits that help us produce our own moments of kindness.

Bear in mind that the bee which makes the honey lives upon a bitter food; and in like manner we can never make acts of gentleness and patience, or gather the honey of the truest virtues, better than while eating the bread of bitterness and enduring hardness. And just as the best honey is that made from thyme, a small and bitter herb, so that virtue which is practiced amid bitterness and lowly sorrow is the best of all virtues.[4]

Recognizing Moments of Kindness

Though kindness reflects inner stability and consistency, its manifestation is episodic. It occurs in specific incidents—moments of kindness and acts of generosity. When one person listens intently and cares deeply about another's discomfort, the inner experience of kindness is shown in a specific interaction. When someone provides a resource to help someone in need, it's an act of kindness that reflects an inner world of virtue. There are many acts of kindness all around us. They are found in a compliment, a smile, an act of hospitality, an embrace, a phone call, an apology. And when these moments occur frequently in the presence of another, we think of that person as kind.

As I talked with the spouse of a faculty colleague at a social gathering, I mentioned how much I appreciated working with her husband. I wondered how she would respond. Would she tell me he puts on a good act, but he's really not that great of a guy? Would she tell me how smart he is? Would she tell me how hard he works at his career? No. Her response went something like this: "He is such a kind man. I don't know how much he has told you about our past. But when we were married fourteen years ago, we had both known a great deal of pain in the past. He has helped me so much because he is so kind."

Notice two essential elements in this response. First, this marriage appears to be filled with acts of kindness. Second, the kindness is more noticeable because of pain from the past. We notice, and are sometimes amazed by, acts of kindness because they stand in contrast to our customary state of stress that is caused by living in a fallen world.

I remember being stranded on a freeway with an overheated radiator in the middle of a thousand-mile trip to college. As feelings of hopelessness were settling in, a man in a pickup pulled off the road. He had a large water tank in the back of his pickup which he used to help me cool down the car and refill the radiator. I made it to the next town for repairs. It was a generous act under any circumstances, but in my moment of stress it stood out as an act of incredible compassion.

One woman I interviewed described the pain of losing an important relationship. She went on to tell how her friends and family members had overwhelmed her with acts of support and kindness. These go hand in hand. Kindness takes on special significance in times of stress and pain. Stress prepares us to recognize and value moments of kindness.

Obstacles to Perceiving Kindness
You may be thinking of exceptions, as I am. We all know those for whom stress has fermented into bitterness. Some have difficulty seeing kindness. We strain to see kindness, but there are common obstacles that sometimes make it difficult to perceive.

When I arrived at my office one morning, I noticed a voice mail message from my friend and colleague Jim. Phone propped at my ear, I turned on my computer and shuffled a few papers as I listened to his message, preparing myself for a full day with an overstuffed agenda. Jim knew nothing of the stress I had faced during the past twenty-four hours—an aching interpersonal stress that had kept me awake half the night. But Jim knows a great deal about the spiritual life. His closing words calmed my spirit and lifted my eyes to see kindness. They were simple words, not profound, but overflowing with kindness: "I hope this message finds you well, and I'm glad you're here at Wheaton. And take care, enjoy your family and know of the Lord's warm embrace and words of affirmation." As I heard those words of kindness, I felt peace and comfort settle over me; I was ready for a great day.

Jim's simple words provided a moment of kindness in my time of need. I fear there are many other times when we miss these simple moments of kindness because we are too relaxed, too stressed, too cynical. These are obstacles to recognizing moments of kindness.

Obstacle 1: Too Relaxed

Problems with stress almost always occur at the extremes. One may conclude, The less stress I have, the better off I will be. This is one extreme. As appealing as this may sound, it is not true. Those who know no stress are poorly prepared to know kindness. As a page on my desk calendar proclaims, "Leisure is a beautiful garment, but it will not do for constant wear."

Imagine becoming the proud parent of a new baby boy who comes with a manual containing the following instructions:

Your baby is a gift and should be treated as a precious gift at all times. Stress will hurt your child, so be careful not to expose him to stressful circumstances. During the infancy years, you should never let your baby cry. Rock him, feed him, coddle him, but never let him cry.

As a toddler, your child needs to learn confidence. Be sure not to crush his spirit by saying no. Also, be sure he never hurts himself. Watch him at all times. Accidents cause stress.

During his grade-school years, make sure he gets everything he wants. Drive him to school, say yes to his every request, do his homework with him, and never punish him, because punishment causes stress.

As a teenager, he will need resources for independence. Give him a car as soon as he turns sixteen. Provide insurance for him, because working while going to school would add too much stress. Continue helping him with his homework. Let him set the rules of the household to build his confidence as a leader. Remember, no stress.

These instructions spell disaster! What happens to the child who faces no demands or stresses in life? We call the child spoiled. He or she can't recognize kindness and only learns to exploit the goodwill of others. The term *spoiled* has become trite, almost a cliché, because it has been used so frequently. When we open the refrigerator door and find that once-tasty leftovers have spoiled, we feel disappointed. How much more should we grieve when a human child is spoiled by overindulgence?

When children receive immunizations for polio, mumps, measles and other childhood diseases, they are injected with a small amount of the virus that causes these diseases. Their immune systems then develop antibodies to fight the infections they might later be exposed to. Stress inoculation works in a similar way. As children learn to experience small amounts of stress, often in response to the choices they make, they learn to cope with later stress.

How do pampered children develop? They often expect, rather than appreciate, acts of kindness. They cannot know mercy without knowing something about standards of justice. They cannot know grace without experiencing neediness. They cannot recognize kindness without knowing about accountability and responsibility.

It's fairly safe to talk about parenting and children, but do we ever pamper ourselves in similar ways? How often do we assume that we shouldn't have to deal with stress, that life ought to be easy, that relationships should always work out, that money should be available when we need it and that the best things in life are the ones that bring the most pleasure?

Two things happen when we believe in the fantasy of stressless living. First, we ultimately fail and become bitter. Credit cards, vacations and transitory relationships may relieve stress for a time but often create enormous stress later. Second, we lose perspective and fail to see the small acts of kindness all around us. When we spend our time telling ourselves, "I deserve better," we become absorbed in our bitterness and neglect taking time to see the beauty, the moments of kindness, all around. Even if we could somehow succeed and find the stressless life, we still would find it difficult to recognize kindness because there would be little need for kindness in a world filled with ease.

Obstacle 2: Too Stressed
Some take on too much stress. Constant stress prevents us from knowing kindness because stress narrows our focus of attention, as discussed previously.

We should be grateful that stress narrows our thinking. The stress of crossing a busy street causes the young schoolchild to think only about looking both ways. The stress of learning to drive causes the sixteen-year-old to invest enormous thinking energy into the task at hand (at least we hope so). Adults succeed in their work as they allow stress to help them concentrate and focus.

Though the stress response is good, remember that it is not meant to stay in the "on" position constantly. We also need time for reflection, relaxation and relief. Sometimes in the midst of our daily hassles, we forget to turn off the stress.

As my oldest daughter and I walked into the local McDonald's recently, we saw the icon of contemporary life. It was a man sitting by himself, eating fast food, reading a newspaper and talking on his cellular phone—all at the same time. When I mentioned my surprise to Danielle, she didn't understand. What was so unusual about an efficient McDonald's patron?

Then I realized that this is the pace she has always known. Hers is the generation of saying yes to every opportunity. She is one who put a one-dollar bill in my Christmas stocking along with a note: "Sorry—no time—buy yourself a candy bar and keep the change for retirement." My generation is overwhelmed with stress. I wonder what will happen to hers.

In the midst of all this stress, our thinking remains narrow, focused on survival and success. Narrowed thinking is helpful in the midst of stress, but it also keeps us from looking around and recognizing moments of kindness. We need breaks from stress in order to see kindness.

Remember the adage "Take time to smell the roses"? We can get so focused and preoccupied with stress that we don't even know where the nearest roses are. The problem isn't stress. The problem is constant stress. There's no time to recognize kindness in a life crammed full of hassles and pressures.

Obstacle 3: Too Cynical

Human kindness is "overflowing." Bette Midler sang these words in the movie *Beaches*. But it's easy to question Bette's tuneful assertion. If human kindness were really overflowing, would we live in the midst of global conflict, starvation, crime, racism and broken relationships? Doesn't it make more sense to say that human kindness is dried up or dripping slowly? Is there even such a thing as kindness, or is it just a thinly disguised way of currying people's favor? Such cynical thoughts as these keep us from appreciating moments of kindness.

Imagine the following situation: You're walking alone down a city street when you come across two grade-school boys who are obviously angry with each other. As you approach, the smaller child begins to hit the bigger one. What would be a kind action? Would you do it? If so, why?

Social scientists (perhaps the greatest cynics of all) have come up with theories to explain acts of altruism and kindness. Many of us might not help at all, especially if others are around also.[5] Those of us choosing not to help would have to justify our actions, so we might reason that the bigger child is simply getting what he deserves. Social psychologists call this the "just world assumption." When we observe others suffering, we often assume they are getting what they deserve.

This phenomenon was first noticed by a social psychologist working at a medical school. Melvin Lerner, the psychologist, noticed that medical students didn't want to work with poor patients. In fact, the medical students made critical comments about the indigent, stating that they were poor because they lacked initiative and willpower.[6] Lerner began researching the phenomenon and found that all of us, not just medical students, are prone to think this way. We start with the assumption that the world is fair and then judge the misfortunes of others based on that assumption. In one study participants observed an innocent volunteer receive painful shocks (actually the volunteer was an actor who only pretended to receive the shocks). When the shocks ended, many of those observing were critical of the volunteer, reasoning, "She got what she deserved."[7] The just world assumption explains why rape victims are often blamed and told, "You should have known better!"[8] It's why many needy people don't get much help. We so easily assume that people are needy because of personal choices they have made. Does it really make sense to sing that human kindness is overflowing?

And what if we did stop to help the fighting children? Does this mean we are kind and compassionate? Not necessarily. Social scientists have also developed theories as to why we sometimes act altruistically.

One theory for why people act kindly is that they compute a quick cost-reward analysis and decide that it is good for themselves.[9] We feel anxious when we see these children fighting, and we continue feeling anxious if we ignore the problem and keep on walking. But intervening brings the risk of embarrassment or disapproval from the children. Which risk is greater? According to this cost-reward theory, our brain does a quick computation as to which response would best reduce our anxiety; then we respond accordingly. The problem is that this theory reduces kindness to selfishness: "I'll be kind if it's best for me." This cynical view keeps us from recognizing moments of true kindness.

A second possibility is presented by sociobiology. It suggests that our behavior is determined by past evolution and designed to enhance our species's chance of survival. Sociobiologists believe we all come preprogrammed to preserve and expand the human gene pool. Any behavior is evaluated by whether it perpetuates life and reproduction. Self-sacrificial altruism does not occur, they claim, unless it perpetuates the species (for example, caring for our children helps them survive long enough to reproduce). More cynicism.

These social science theories have interesting evidence to support them, and we must be careful not to dismiss them rashly. But isn't there more to human kindness than can be reduced to simple theories of cost-reward analysis or sociobiology? Isn't there something deeply spiritual about moments of kindness that transcends field studies and laboratory experiments?

Cynical theories don't explain kindness any more than dry, brittle leaves explain botany. Many parts of our human nature are dry and crusty. But there is more. We are also created in God's image and made to thrive in relationships, so we have deep inner longings to give and receive kindness. Most, when faced with a rape victim, don't say, "You got what you deserved." Instead, we feel empathy or compassion, and many reach out to help. How are we to understand those Christians who hid Jews in their homes during the Holocaust? And what about the many thousands of people who volunteer time to renovate homes for Habitat for Humanity, or the millions who give to charities for hunger relief, shelters for the homeless, racial reconciliation and so on? Maybe human kindness does overflow in certain people in certain places at certain times.

Defining Moments
Two things are essential to seeing kindness in the world around us. One is

enough stress to recognize kindness when we see it, and the other is a caring relationship. Kindness is a team sport—it cannot be known outside of relationships.

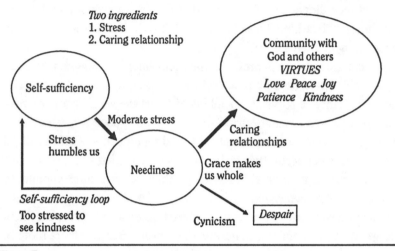

Figure 7

When Jim left the voice mail message for me on that busy morning, I was prepared to experience kindness. If it were a stressless day (is there such a day?), his words would have fallen on deaf ears. I might have said to myself, *That's a nice message. I wonder what novel I should read today.* And if I had no relationship with Jim, I would have thought he was weird. May I know the Lord's warm embrace? Who is this guy, a telephone evangelist? Am I supposed to punch in my VISA number now? But because I felt stressed, and because I knew and respected Jim, his message was brimming with kindness.

The central message of Christian thought requires these same two elements. We are stressed, desperate, weak people in need of help. God demonstrates the greatest kindness by entering into relationship with us through Jesus Christ.

For while we were still weak, at the right time Christ died for the ungodly. Indeed, rarely will anyone die for a righteous person—though perhaps for a good person someone might actually dare to die. But God proves his love for us in that while we still were sinners Christ died for us. (Romans 5:6-8)

There will be no greater kindness. But those who don't know their stressed, needy condition and those who refuse relationship with Christ can never know the kindness of God.

Character That Produces Kindness

Recognizing kindness is one thing; producing it is another. I am particularly interested in the role of faith in the process of learning to produce kindness. If God's light keeps us from being dry and brittle in spirit and draws us toward kindness, then it makes sense that Christians set the standards for empathy, generosity and love. In fact, I can't imagine a better way to transform our troubled, stressed world than by participating in what author Steve Sjogren calls a "conspiracy of kindness."[10]

And fortunately, some research evidence suggests that faith does make a difference. Those deeply committed to religious faith are more likely than others to show kindness.[11]

Right about now you may be thinking of exceptions to this rule as your mind gravitates toward examples of selfishness, greed, mindless ambition and pettiness that seem so common, even among committed Christians. Yes, the church is made up of fallen, broken people, and it is easy to find examples of sin. But there is also reason for hope.

When evangelicals split from the so-called social gospel early in the twentieth century, they lost ground in kindness as they made progress in doctrinal purity. Now many Christians are trying to reconstruct a responsible evangelicalism that seems to be slowly emerging from the rubble of human divisiveness. Nowadays Christians can believe in the authority of Scripture and still care about homelessness, poverty, ethnic inequities and world hunger.[12] We have hope because we know the Creator of kindness, and we know enough about stress and our own fallen nature to empathize with those who need kindness the most.

A Personal Matter

We also must recognize that kindness does not happen primarily on an institutional level. Kindness occurs on a personal level. Imagine moving to a new neighborhood, hearing a knock on your new front door, opening it and hearing the following: "Hello, I'm with Welcome Incorporated. We provide welcoming services for neighborhoods all over America. Your neighbors subscribe to our service and have contracted with us to provide one meal for each new family in the neighborhood. Would you like the lasagna or the veal?" This would be an act of kindness, but it would feel very different from having a new neighbor from across the street bring a home-cooked meal.

Kindness is an inner state that reveals itself in relationships. If we are to be transformed into kind people, it must happen within our character instead of within our institutions. But how?

Personal kindness can't be put on like a coat. It comes from a deep personal understanding of our neediness and kindness that has been shown to us. Jesus told a parable of a slave and a king:

For this reason the kingdom of heaven may be compared to a king who wished to settle accounts with his slaves. When he began the reckoning, one who owed him ten thousand talents was brought to him; and, as he could not pay, his lord ordered him to be sold, together with his wife and children and all his possessions, and payment to be made. So the slave fell on his knees before him, saying, "Have patience with me, and I will pay you everything." And out of pity for him, the lord of that slave released him and forgave him the debt. But that same slave, as he went out, came upon one of his fellow slaves who owed him a hundred denarii; and seizing him by the throat, he said, "Pay what you owe." Then his fellow slave fell down and pleaded with him, "Have patience with me, and I will pay you." But he refused; then he went and threw him into prison until he would pay the debt. (Matthew 18:23-30)

Of course the king became very upset and handed over the first slave to torture until he could pay the debt. This story, filled with hyperbole, illustrates how much forgiveness and kindness God has shown us. This slave owed his king ten thousand talents—an unimaginable amount of money—yet he demanded payment of the relatively small amount owed him by a fellow slave. The message is striking. Once we understand our neediness and the immeasurable kindness that has been shown us, how can we keep from showing kindness to our neighbors? Personal kindness reflects self-awareness and spiritual devotion more than willpower or "putting on" a nice persona.

Putting on Kindness

Every year as October rolls around, parents in America hear the same question from their children: "What can I be this year?" Somehow the parents and their children always figure it out, and on October 31 all kinds of unusual and surprising faces show up seeking candy at our front doors.

What is so compelling about Halloween? What makes children lie awake at night wondering whether to be a cheerleader, a politician, a vampire or a Walt Disney character? The obvious answer is candy. But if candy were the only motivator, parents would soon figure out that it is much cheaper and quicker to buy a couple of pounds of candy than to buy the hip Halloween outfit and walk from door to door with Frankenstein Jr. or the Little Mermaid.

How would it go over in your house? You could walk into the house on October 1 with a shopping bag full of candy, dump it on the dining-room table and announce to the kids that this year the candy will be freely given—they don't have to worry about costumes, crossing dark streets or walking from door to door. A few hours after the candy is consumed, a timid voice would probably be heard asking, "What can I be this year?"

A child's intrigue with Halloween goes beyond satisfying a sweet tooth. Halloween provides a chance to "put on" a different character. It's the same intrigue we adults have with theater or reading a novel. We can put ourselves in a different role and see what it might be like—a make-believe character to cloak our feelings of uncertainty.

The same phenomenon might happen in reading this book. The characteristics of love, joy, peace, patience and kindness sound appealing and inviting. We might decide to try on kindness like a new coat. We may even picture ourselves acting with unusual kindness toward our loved ones and associates. But these pictures may fade in the crucible of human relationships, especially those that are difficult.

Putting on kindness is a noble image that reflects willpower and a sincere desire to change. The apostle Paul instructed believers to "put on" the Lord

Jesus Christ (Romans 13:14) and to "put on" the whole armor of God (Ephesians 6:11). In this sense, we ought to put on kindness.

But in another sense, kindness can't be put on. Becoming kind is not as easy as putting on a costume or playing a role. A desire to become kind, even a strong desire coupled with willpower, is not enough. Kindness is forged in our character as we recognize our own need for kindness through the difficult days of life, and as we see and practice kindness in relation to others.

Stress and Kindness Need Each Other

In our self-help society, it is easy to assume that change occurs through obtaining the right information or implementing proper strategies. Learning kindness is not so simple.

We recognize kindness because we know stress. To understanding this, think about the balance of stress and kindness in rearing children. The example given earlier in this chapter illustrated what kind of child an "all kindness/no stress" policy might produce. But the other extreme, "high stress/low kindness," is no better. Kids raised in harsh, cold environments don't learn kindness because they don't experience it and don't see it modeled for them. The healthiest homes are those in which children experience minor stress but have ample supplies of kindness to help them along ("high kindness/moderate stress"). Stress helps us recognize kindness, and kindness helps us cope with stress.

Is there hope for children from "all kindness/no stress" homes? Yes, once they experience stress. Children from sheltered homes cannot avoid stress forever. They walk out of the house at age eighteen and get knocked over by stress. They drag themselves to their feet and get knocked over again. After it happens over and over, they start to learn that kindness is a gift from others, not something they can demand or expect.

Is there hope for children from "high stress/low kindness" homes? Yes, but it comes in the form of a relationship in which kindness is displayed. A caring teacher, a supportive coach, an empathic psychotherapist or a gentle pastor can help teach kindness to those who have seen little at home. Stress and kindness need each other.

We can put on kindness in a variety of situations, but the kindness that results from transformed character requires stress. "Kindness is only tested and can only mature when it faces unkindness."[13] One person responded to my questions about stress this way: "I honestly believe that we do *not* grow as Christians unless and until we experience suffering and pain." He went on to describe how his fears of career failure have deepened his empathy and kindness for others and have prompted him to encourage others. I believe he is right: kindness and stress need each other.

Awareness Exercise

Think of the greatest failure in your life. Undoubtedly it's an unpleasant memory, and you would never choose to live through it again. But how has that experience allowed you to understand kindness differently? How did you see kindness from others? How have you learned to be kind to those in need? We are fragile people who need one another. Kindness thrives in the midst of stress and caring relationships.

8

Generosity

*A person first starts to live
when he can live outside of himself.*
ALBERT EINSTEIN[1]

Most of us want to be generous, but translating our desires into actions can be difficult. Consider the following common situations.

Just as you're sitting down to enjoy a hot meal with your family after a long, stressful day, the phone rings. You recognize immediately that it is a sales call, because the caller mispronounces your name. It's another call for aluminum siding or credit card protection services or a brand-new travel club. As you wait to get in a word, just a little two-letter word that starts with *N,* your hot meal is crying out to you, "Come to me." Eventually the salesperson takes a breath, and you jump in with "No, thank you."

What does it mean to be generous? Saying yes to every phone sales opportunity would bankrupt most of us. Can a person be generous in saying no?

You sit back down and sink your fork into a great-looking quiche. As it approaches your lips, you hear the doorbell chime. What now? Standing at your door is a neighbor child raising money to help the middle-school volleyball team by selling candy. She is the third candy salesperson this week, and you're getting tired of caramel-filled chocolate bars. What does it mean to be generous?

By the time you get back to your cold quiche, your patience is wearing thin. Just as you sit down, your child announces, "I'm all done. Can you help me with my algebra homework?" What does it mean to be generous?

Many of us struggle with this same question when we walk the streets of an inner city and are approached by a destitute person asking for spare change. And we may have the same response when we come to a four-way stop and find people at the intersection collecting money for a good cause. And what should we do when a long, slow truck is waiting to pull onto a busy road, and we have a chance to let the truck in? What does it mean to be generous?

Paul included *agathos* among the fruits of the Spirit. *Agathos* is most commonly translated as "goodness," but sometimes as "generosity." Neither word captures the concept perfectly. "Goodness" reminds us of virtuous inner character, and this is an essential part of *agathos*. It connotes a fullness and integrity of character. "Generosity" implies giving to others, and this is also an essential part of *agathos*. But this is a giving that flows from character filled with goodness—generosity from the inside out. The generous person can't stuff all the goodness inside, so it starts overflowing onto others. This kind of generosity goes even deeper than kindness, straight to the heart of a person. *Agathos* refers to the strong, the pure, the sincere, and it springs forth in godlike action toward others.[2]

Of Course Not

Does this mean a generous person says yes to every opportunity? Of course not—for two reasons. First, most of us could simply not afford the time or money that every opportunity would require. Second, we can never measure virtuous character by outward behavior alone. Philosopher Robert Roberts writes, "Generosity does not consist just in giving away one's goods, but in having a certain attitude toward them."[3] Generosity requires us to live with outstretched hands, not clenched and grasping fists. The desire to help, to reach out to those in need, to do kind deeds and say soothing words flows from the character of a generous person. Though no one has the resources to help everyone, a generous person never loses that inner tug to say yes whenever possible.

So what about the sales call for aluminum siding at dinner hour? Generosity causes us to visualize a minimum-wage employee with little opportunity for advancement who may have been personally ridiculed and criticized dozens of times in the previous hour. Generosity means we would like to say yes, just because this phone caller may work on commission. But reality constrains us. If we said yes to every phone sales call, we would also have to say yes to every credit card offer that comes in the mail, and soon our personal debt would approach the national debt! So we say no in most cases, but the generous person says no with some discomfort and a tug of compassion.

A sad result of our psychologized society is that we have often turned human goodness and generosity into pathology. If we decide to say no to the child selling candy bars at our doorstep and tell someone that we feel bad about saying no, we are likely to be called "codependent," "subassertive" or "a people-pleaser." These popular psychology concepts have helped many people toward greater emotional health. But when these concepts start saturating society, people sometimes misapply them and start using them to justify self-centeredness.

Goodness and generosity are virtues, not sicknesses. They are virtues that cannot be contained. They keep spilling out of a healthy inner life and flowing over others. Generosity affects more than our finances. It changes our thoughts, our speech and our emotional responses. Goodness goes with us to the office and to the supermarket and waits with us in traffic jams. It helps us raise our children, talk with angry customers and coach the Little League team.

Does stress create generosity? Not automatically, but stress teaches us empathy, and empathy helps us develop goodness. When goodness overflows, it becomes generosity. Do you find yourself feeling irritated toward slow truckers on busy roads? Try this: drive a large U-Haul across the country. This experience is sure to produce empathy for and generosity toward truck drivers. Tragedy often produces the same result. Many parents whose children have been killed by drunk drivers become advocates for other parents whose children have not yet been hurt. Rape victims become peer counselors to help other victims. Stress creates empathy, and empathy fuels goodness and generosity.

What does it mean to be generous? The specific answer is often defined by the stress in our lives.

An Act of Grace

When most people think of generosity, they think in human-centered terms. They understand generosity as an act of human goodness, an indicator of the noble qualities of humanity. Generosity is initiated by humans and affirms humanistic ideals. But when Christians think of generosity, we think in God-centered terms.[4] The Christian sees generosity as evidence of God's nature more than human nature. Generosity is initiated by God in response to our brokenness and neediness. Human generosity, to the Christian, is a reflection of divine grace.

I love the juxtaposition of Psalm 40 and Psalm 41. At the end of Psalm 40 (v. 17), David writes of his neediness before God: "As for me, I am poor and needy, but the LORD takes thought for me. You are my help and my deliverer; do not delay, O my God."

David is crying out to God for divine generosity. But the next psalm, also written by David (41:1-3), begins with a description of human generosity.

Happy are those who consider the poor;
    the LORD delivers them in the day of trouble.
The LORD protects them and keeps them alive;
    they are called happy in the land.
You do not give them up to the will of their enemies.
The LORD sustains them on their sickbed;
    in their illness you heal all their infirmities.

Together these psalms show the Christian image of generosity. In our need we call out for God, who delivers us. How else, then, can we respond to the needs of others? Generosity is a natural extension of God's grace toward us.

So stress and generosity go together for the Christian. Stress humbles us and makes us aware of our needy, sinful state, like Saul when he was ambushed and blinded on the road to Damascus (see Acts 9). God restores us by freely granting us divine vision and then calls us to be generous to others.

Working with the Spirit

The apostle Paul writes that the fruit of the Spirit is "love, joy, peace, patience, kindness, generosity . . ." (Galatians 5:22-23). God often uses stress as a tool to produce these fruits in us (see Romans 5:3-5; James 1:2-4). Stress humbles us so grace can make us whole through the work of the Holy Spirit.

Stephen Winward suggests four means by which we can work with the Holy Spirit to produce fruit: attention, devotion, restraint and practice.[5] All four are tools that help virtue emerge from a life filled with stress, including virtues such as goodness and generosity.

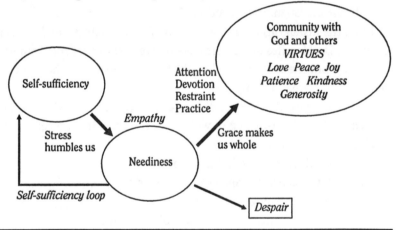

Figure 8

Attention

First, we help the Spirit produce fruit by paying attention to spiritual matters. Generosity, for example, can only occur when we pay attention to the needs around us. The person who sees a need and gives willingly to meet that need, even before being asked to help, has exercised both attention and generosity. For example, a group of Christians may recognize the needs of a family in great stress and decide to provide meals for that family for a period of time. Each meal will probably be received as a gift of love. If that same family had called the church and said, "We're in need—can someone please provide meals for us?" the response, though still generous, would feel different.

Although I agree with Winward that paying attention to God helps produce the fruit of the Spirit, I am also aware that this is easier to talk about than to do. It's so easy to let our attention drift. One of the most common psychological disorders in children is called attention deficit disorder (ADD). Those with ADD have difficulty concentrating and focusing on the task at hand. Attention deficit disorder is a fitting analogy for our spiritual condition. Working with the Holy Spirit requires us to pay attention to spiritual matters, but it is common to let the spiritual life get buried under the clutter of life in the information age. We try to concentrate on the spiritual by attending church, having personal devotions, listening to Christian music and so on, but it is so easy to drift away—spiritual attention deficit.

Does our attention drift because we lack interest? This is no more accurate than saying the ADD child doesn't have enough willpower to concentrate on a math assignment. Just as the ADD child is fighting many learned and biological forces, so we all are fighting our fallen nature that affects spiritual functioning.

Stress, as unpleasant as it feels, is often God's way of recapturing our attention. When life gets too easy, too comfortable, we may settle into our routines without noticing the profound needs all around us. Stress moves us out of our comfort zone and causes us to pay attention to the needs around us.

Devotion

A second way we help the Spirit produce fruit is through private and public acts of devotion. If we are devoted to God, we will spend time worshiping, conversing with and gratefully recalling the deeds of God. Devotion aligns us with God's ways and allows the Spirit to produce fruit.

Stress is an essential component of devotion. What can a husband and wife know about devotion to each other until their love is tested with stress?

These are the elements of virtually every love story ever told: Boy meets girl. Boy and girl fall deeply in love. Some enormous stressor disrupts the relationship. Boy and girl prove themselves faithful and devoted. They live happily ever after.

Our devotion to God is tested, even defined, by our response in times of stress. As we remain devoted to God, the Holy Spirit continues to produce fruit in our lives, including the fruit of generosity.

It is one thing to be good and generous when life is relatively easy, and a more difficult thing to be good and generous when life is hard. Offering a cheerful word to another when we ourselves are filled with feelings of pressure and fear is an act of true generosity. Giving financially when our own personal financial state is troubled and uncertain is an act of generosity and devotion.

Restraint

Allowing the Spirit's fruit in our life also requires restraint. Every fiber of human character is tainted by sin, which means that our perceptions are self-centered, our desires distorted, our ways deceitful. In stark contrast, Jesus entered the world with purity of focus and divine nature. Jesus, in his goodness, cared for the poor. We, in our sinfulness, ignore the poor and think about what color our next car should be. Jesus worked to reconcile people of different backgrounds and values. We often segregate ourselves and justify our actions by claiming the world is just, or that the government is taking care of ethnic reconciliation. Jesus hated sin. We flirt with it. Jesus came to transform us so that we can live in light rather than darkness. Sometimes we choose darkness.

We can never save ourselves through mere effort, but once Christ saves us from our darkness, we help the Spirit transform us by deliberately restraining our selfish desires. Generosity requires restraint in the midst of our stress. Taking time to listen to someone in pain is a generous act that requires restraint. Giving money to someone in need restrains us from using that money for personal desires. Showing kindness to a marginalized person requires us to restrain our natural desire for safety and predictability. To be generous, we must restrain our natural inclinations to please ourselves.

Saying no to our natural desires is stressful. If our primary goal is to reduce stress, then we must please ourselves and avoid generosity. But if our goal is to live transformed lives, even if stress is a side effect, then we must train ourselves to say no to our selfish desires and yes to others.

Awareness Exercise

Training ourselves to say no is an ongoing challenge. Unless it is medically unwise, try the spiritual discipline of fasting for a day. Each time you feel hungry, remind yourself that you are in training, just as an athlete trains for an important competition. You are learning to say no to yourself as you train for this virtue of restraint.

Practice

Finally, we work with the Spirit by practicing the virtues and spiritual disciplines. Practice, of course, is stressful. My high-school football coach wasn't content with daily doubles, so we had three practices a day. He told us every day that we would be the best-conditioned team in the state of Oregon. Practice was stressful. But as we dressed for the state playoffs several months later, none of us was complaining.

We cannot know how to pray or act in a moment of crisis unless we have prepared ourselves with hours of practice. Daily hassles provide the practice field for our spiritual life. When a driver cuts us off on the freeway or a grocery line moves too slowly or a computer crashes, we can practice a virtuous response. Early in the morning, when there is time for solitude and prayer, we can practice the spiritual disciplines.

Practicing virtue shapes our character, just as practicing a cross-body block shapes a football player's skills. Even those not prone to generosity can become generous with practice. Practice is at the heart of generosity. Each time we give our time, effort and money, we learn more about generosity.

Here the relationship between inner qualities of goodness and outer acts of generosity may appear confusing. If generosity spills over from an inner life crammed with goodness, then why would we need practice? Won't we be naturally generous just by focusing on inner virtue? The answer is found in the bi-directional connection between goodness and generosity. Transformed character makes us more generous, and practicing generous acts helps transform our character.

Think about smiling, for example. We are more prone to smile, an outward behavior, when we are happy inside. But it is also true that we are more inclined to feel happy when we are smiling.[6] In fact, those who are forced to smile while reading cartoons rate the cartoons as funnier than those who are forced to frown while reading the same cartoons.[7] Our inner state affects our smiling behavior, and our smiling behavior affects our inner state. In the same way, our inner qualities of goodness affect our capacity to be generous, and practicing generosity affects our inner character qualities. Each time we give generously, we invest in our own maturity as well as the charity we have selected.

An Empathy Bridge

Generosity that flows from inner goodness requires us to find a common denominator with those in need—empathy. Empathy causes us to enter another's world to get a fresh perspective on his or her experiences. How would I respond to the problem of homelessness if I myself had been homeless? How would you respond to world hunger if one of your children had starved to death? How would we vote if we really understood the challenges of the inner city?

Our desire for prosperity often impedes empathy and causes us to direct our energies toward accumulating rather than giving. When we have silver dollars covering our eyes, we can't see others clearly. Donald Hinze, a minister and author of *To Give and Give Again,* writes: "Our preoccupation with getting and spending is destroying our awareness of God, who is within us."[8] The apostle Paul said something similar to Timothy:

> For the love of money is a root of all kinds of evil, and in their eagerness to be rich some have wandered away from the faith and pierced themselves with many pains. But as for you, man of God, shun all this; pursue righteousness, godliness, faith, love, endurance, gentleness. (1 Timothy 6:10-11)

Empathy forces us beyond a "getting" mentality and toward a gracious God who calls us to live in community with one another.

What is the relationship between stress and generosity? Stress gives us opportunities for empathy, and empathy produces goodness and generosity. Generosity, in turn, enhances community. "Giving develops an interpersonal ethic that promotes fellowship within the human family. When we empathize with others—sharing emotions and possessions—we experience an inner peace and freedom from loneliness."[9]

In describing to me his greatest life stressors, one person stated, "Difficult times have given me greater empathy for all persons." Stress can do this for us. It humbles us so that we can really listen to and understand one another. And then, in the context of our Christian communities, we can generously lift one another up to experience the fruit of God's Spirit. "The faithful will abound with blessings, but one who is in a hurry to be rich will not go unpunished" (Proverbs 28:20).

9

Faithfulness

May all who come behind us find us faithful.
STEVE GREEN

A spiritual mentor once told me, "Don't just do something. Stand there!" How can we learn to stand still, to be faithful? By living in a life filled with turbulence. In such a life most of us have ample opportunity to practice faithfulness.

For the title of his book on the psalms of ascent, Eugene Peterson borrowed the phrase *A Long Obedience in the Same Direction* from a German philosopher and then added the subtitle *Discipleship in an Instant Society.*[1] What a wise and wonderful goal: to walk faithfully through life, just as the Jewish people made the long upward journey to Jerusalem three times each year. As the pilgrims walked along, they sang songs that we now call the ascent psalms (Psalms 120—134). Can you picture them singing? "Those who trust in the LORD are like Mount Zion, which cannot be moved, but abides forever" (Psalm 125:1). They are singing about faithfulness: Don't just do something. Stand there like Mount Zion.

Faithfulness is learned and demonstrated in the hot, uphill climbs of life, like that journey to Jerusalem. We might prefer to learn faithfulness by sipping lemonade while lying in a hammock on a tropical island. But the reality is that we learn faithfulness by changing diapers, taking children to recitals, working through differences with ones we love and giving money.

Of Course Not

Does this mean that stress and temptation always make us faithful people? Of course not. Stress often precipitates tremendous problems. Stress is a flash point that brings about greater faithfulness or irresponsibility.

David has been overwhelmed with stress. Demands at work have been escalating, he has been arguing with Janet more, and the kids are having problems in school. He feels overwhelmed with responsibilities and inadequate to meet the demands that surround him. One of his coworkers has expressed an attraction toward him. Next week they are going out of town together on business.

Chris promised Robert she would make it to his next Little League game. Her recent promotion has added tremendous pressure at work, and she feels torn between her desires to be a good parent and a good executive. The game starts at 5:30 p.m. As the hour hand creeps beyond the 5 and the minute hand sweeps past the 12, Chris is pushed toward a choice.

What will David do? What will Chris do? In one sense, the stress works against a wise choice. Under other circumstances David might have no problem keeping an appropriate distance from his coworker. The stress makes him vulnerable. Similarly, Chris would normally make it to her son's game, but this evening it's different because of the stress she is facing.

Stress defines faithfulness, just as an earthquake defines excellent engineering and construction. If David chooses to remain faithful to Janet, and if Chris makes it to Robert's game, they have demonstrated faithfulness in spite of stress. The kind of faithfulness we want is the kind that stands up to stress tests. If we're not tested, how can we know we are faithful? Stress defines our faithfulness.

Educators often comment that the worst thing about their job is giving exams and assigning grades. But we keep doing it for a reason: a good test helps students learn essential skills. Each fall I teach a psychometrics class to first-year doctoral students (psychometrics is the study of testing and measurement and involves complex conceptual and mathematical concepts). Students coming to Wheaton College for a doctorate in psychology are rarely studying psychology because they love mathematical theory. Thus many concepts in the class are difficult for them to grasp, and most students suffer and complain during the first weeks of the course. They tell themselves things like *I will never survive this class* and *If this is psychology, I made the wrong choice.* As the midterm exam approaches, the stress levels climb even higher. I am surrounded by bloodshot eyes and looks of hostility as I hand out the take-home exams. But as I collect the exams a week later, the strangest thing happens. Most of the students come back smiling, saying, "I finally understand this stuff." From that point forward, they understand and enjoy the class.

As much as educators dislike testing and assigning grades, there are times when students learn best through testing. Sometimes the reading, discussing and classroom examples don't help as much as facing a test. So it is with faithfulness. We learn to be faithful through the stresses, trials and tests of life. No other way works quite as well.

Does stress automatically make us faithful? Of course not. But we can learn faithfulness best in times of stress.

How We Are Faithful

When writing about faithfulness, it is tempting to cite statistics about divorce, extramarital affairs, child abandonment and so on because these major life traumas illustrate how unfaithfulness hurts people. But I resist this temptation because these statistics mislead us into thinking that faithfulness is defined by the big problems in life. For example, how do we respond to the question, Have you been faithful in your marriage? Most of us reflexively answer yes, assuming the question is about sexual fidelity. Sexual faithfulness is essential for healthy marriages, but faithfulness is also revealed in the little decisions of life. It affects the things we say about our spouses in public. It means we make the bed or empty the dishwasher even when it isn't our turn. It means we listen when we're tired, we care when we're feeling our own pain too, we are kind when we are angry. Faithfulness is more practical—much more relevant to everyday life—than we imply when we relegate the term to sexual behavior. Faithfulness in little things helps define our character.

How do we learn and demonstrate faithfulness in everyday life? Here are several examples from an almost endless list of possibilities.

Example 1: Kid stuff. Parents have many opportunities for faithfulness, too many it sometimes seems. Just as you're drifting off to sleep, your newborn decides to wake up. At that moment you're probably not thankful for another chance to be a faithful parent. Or what about changing diapers? Children give us a regular (pun intended) opportunity for faithful parenting.

The challenges of childrearing change as kids grow. I remember feeling some relief when our youngest was out of diapers. But just a short while later one of our children burst into our bedroom in the middle of the night. I sat straight up in bed, exclaiming, "Are you OK?" My daughter opened her mouth (presumably to answer my question) and threw up all over our bed. It was a chance for faithful parenting.

Then there is the taxi phase. While the freeways are crowded with commuters, the side roads are filled with suburban parents driving their children to and from various activities in the family minivan. During the gasoline shortage of the 1970s we lowered the speed limit to fifty-five miles per hour in order to save fuel. We should have canceled Little League and piano lessons instead.

All these parenting tasks teach us to be faithful to our children—aware of their needs, sensitive to their personalities, supportive of their dreams. It is the sum of these little acts of faithfulness that equals security in a child's life.

Example 2: Returning phone calls. Recently our family was awakened in the middle of the night by a ringing phone. When I answered it, I realized it was a fax machine with the wrong number. It's hard to persuade a caller to try a different number when all the caller says is "Beep, beep, beep." So I hung up, fully aware of what would happen. Sure enough, five minutes later the fax machine called again. And again. Isn't technology—particularly automatic redial—wonderful?

What comes easy for the fax machine—reaching out and touching someone—is more difficult for most humans in the midst of busy work and family schedules. Most of us have answering machines or voice mail, which means we have more phone calls to return than ever before. Do we return calls?

Each time we return a phone call without hope of a fun or profitable conversation, we exercise faithfulness. And exercise makes a trait grow stronger.

Example 3: Listening. Walking in the door at home after a long day's work, I am greeted by the chatter of energetic family members. "Can Susan spend the night Friday?" "I got a B- on my science test!" "My game starts in forty-five minutes; will dinner be ready soon?" This is a time for faithfulness. Our natural instincts are to escape. I sometimes escape by grabbing the mail and flipping through bills, credit card offers and advertisements. And it works! Before I know it, nobody is talking to me. And then I remember how much my children need to keep talking to me during these adolescent years. The pile of mail suddenly seems trivial.

We train ourselves to be faithful by being available and listening intently. Sometimes we have special opportunities to listen beyond simple words and to hear the deep pain of another. We are trusted with others' pain only after we have proven ourselves faithful listeners.

Example 4: Paying bills. According to that authoritative source of information from the mid-1980s, Trivial Pursuit, sex and money are the source of most marital disputes. Sex and faithfulness have obvious connections, but what about money? Financial stress is a part of life for most of us. We have purchased the American dream, and now we pay for it every month.

Each time we sit down to pay bills, it is as an act of faithfulness. Every time we write checks for the electric bill instead of buying that new sweater at the mall, we act faithfully by fulfilling our promise to our local utility company. Every rent or mortgage payment makes us wait longer to replace the old car, but it also reinforces a lifestyle of faithfulness. Each time we write a check to the local church, a mission or a world relief organization, we learn more about faithfulness.

Example 5: Recycling. Rhetoric about saving the earth fascinates me because the earth will probably survive longer than any of us, whether or not it supports life. The creatures of the earth are fragile—the earth is not. Saving the earth is a euphemism for saving ourselves, our children and their children by saving the earth's resources.

It is a hassle taking off the bottoms of metal cans, smashing them for recycling, sorting plastics by the little numbers inside the familiar triangle and separating newspapers from magazines. Recycling probably takes fifteen minutes each week. But each time we recycle, we learn more about faithfulness to our neighbors throughout the planet and to future generations.

These are just a few examples of practicing faithfulness. There are many more, such as meeting deadlines at work, cooking, maintaining friendships, paying parking tickets, being loyal to family members, tithing, keeping promises and so on. Faithfulness occurs in these daily events. This is where we learn virtue and character so that we can face the big challenges of life with integrity. Jesus put it simply: "Whoever is faithful in a very little is faithful also in much; and whoever is dishonest in a very little is dishonest also in much" (Luke 16:10).

Why We Are Faithful

Motives are at the core of faithfulness. Why do we pay the mortgage instead of buying a new electronic device? Why does a couple remain emotionally and sexually faithful for a lifetime? Why does a parent of a child with special needs remain committed and faithful to that child's care? Why does a friend keep a promise or a confidence? Why does a single parent take on an extra job in order to pay the bills?

Faithfulness as Self-Rewarding Behavior

One possibility is that we are faithful in order to earn something. One prominent social psychological theory, first introduced in chapter seven, suggests we give expecting to receive an equal amount back.[2] This theory reduces faithfulness and other inner virtues to external behaviors. It is a capitalist's free-market view of interpersonal relationships: I give something to you, and you give something to me. Relationships last as long as each person receives about as much as he or she gives. According to this theory, we invest ourselves in others because we get something in exchange from the other person, such as love, status, respect or loyalty. When we don't get back as much as we invest, we perceive the relationship to be unbalanced, and eventually leave the relationship.

I wish I could report that viewing faithfulness as self-rewarding is completely unfounded, but I can't. Various research findings support this theory. For example, one predictor of divorce is "market value." When external standards, such as income potential or physical attractiveness, invest one spouse with greater worth than the other, the one with higher "value" is more likely to leave the relationship, often because of finding a new relationship.

Despite some research support, however, most scholars believe this theory is too cynical and too limited to explain all interpersonal behavior. There are many exceptions—people who are faithful and loyal even when they have nothing to gain. One of the few women to go down with the *Titanic* in 1912 remained calm through the ordeal, helping others board lifeboats. When the lifeboats were almost loaded, her husband, whose physical condition prevented him from being able to board a lifeboat, urged her to enter one. Instead, Isadore Strauss grabbed her husband's arm, placed it against her side and said, "We have been long together through a great many years. We are old now. Where you go, I will go." Simplistic explanations of faithfulness as self-rewarding behavior fail utterly when confronted with people like Isadore Strauss. Viewing faithfulness as a commodity for social exchange robs us of opportunities to grow spiritually and emotionally. When marriage vows are changed from "as long as we both shall *live*" to "as long as we both shall *love*," the opportunity for mature, faithful love is replaced with shallow self-sufficiency. Stress is viewed as a reason to change one relationship for another rather than a mechanism for deepening character. Consider some of the implications of viewing faithfulness as self-rewarding behavior.

Awareness Exercise

As we discuss the three following implications, see if you can find a common problem that is created by viewing faithfulness as self-rewarding behavior. Remember, the question we are asking is, "Why are we faithful to one another?"

Implication 1: Conditional faithfulness—an oxymoron? Jenny starts an ugly rumor about Susan because Susan did not invite Jenny to her birthday party. John slugs Tom in the stomach and pleads to the vice principal, "But he hit me first!" We see examples of conditional faithfulness throughout childhood. It would be nice if we always grew out of childish reasoning, but the same fallenness that plagues children also haunts adults.

Many troubled couples face the same insecurities. One spouse proclaims to the other, "I will be faithful to you as long as you are faithful to me." This is conditional because one uses faithfulness as leverage to control the behavior of another. We might question whether it is faithfulness at all. Or one spouse chooses not to be faithful and then explains it by saying, "I never really loved my spouse." This is conditional because it implies that a promise must be kept only to those we love.

Imagine going to a wedding and listening to these vows: "I promise to forsake all others and love only you, unless it becomes too stressful. If someone more attractive expresses a strong interest in me, or if you are unfaithful to me, then I may not be faithful to you. But otherwise I will be faithful. I promise." This would not make a good foundation for a faithful marriage! Yet these behaviors are common in marriage. Conditional views of faithfulness cause insecurity and uncertainty, produce an intolerance for stress and drive people to extreme behaviors.

Implication 2: Conformity demands. Another implication of viewing faithfulness as a commodity to be earned is an excessive drive toward conformity. If we could get inside the minds of a hundred teenagers, many of them would confuse acceptance with conformity: *I have to dress as others dress. I should use the same words others use. I should love the same social activities others love.*

Why do teenagers struggle with these inner drives for conformity? Isn't it because they expect to be hurt and rejected if they are not perfect? Most of us remember the anxieties of these teenage years when we didn't want to stand out as different. Being different meant being publicly humiliated for wearing pants too short or too long, having too many pimples or wearing the wrong brand of sneakers. The message is clear to a vulnerable teenager: "You are acceptable if . . ." The conditions change with each generation, but the demand is the same.

The same anxieties plague adults, but we just hide them better. Most of us still hate pimples, care too much about the way our hair looks, weigh ourselves compulsively and value certain brands of jeans and shoes above others. Whenever I take my shirt off in the summer, I still worry about my skin being too pale, just as I did in high school. A few years ago I walked into the back yard after dark on a hot summer night. My shirt was off, and the moths fluttered around me. That didn't help my insecurities!

Adults also feel a need to conform. We feel obligated to meet certain middle-class economic standards set by those around us: owning a home, driving a relatively new minivan, having an answering machine and VCR and so on. And there are prestige standards to meet: having an attractive spouse, being promoted every few years, getting frequent flyer miles, wearing dark business suits, having quiet children in church.

Perhaps what we see in teenagers is common to all of us (they are learning it from someone). We often value one another based on how well we conform to certain expectations and norms. Though we don't say it out loud and seldom dare to admit it, perhaps we think in cost-benefit language: I will be valued more if I look like other people; being nice to the boss will help me get promoted; people will think I'm spiritual if I quote Scripture a lot; the neighbors will be upset if my grass gets too tall.

Though these thoughts may sometimes be realistic, conditional views of acceptance make us vulnerable to the harmful effects of stress. The inner life, where faithfulness is learned, is shut out in favor of an external shell of appearance. Virtue takes a back seat to visibility.

Implication 3: Self-sufficiency. When faithfulness is something we expect to earn from or prove to another, we easily slip into the trap of self-sufficiency. Some imagine they will earn faithful love by distinguishing themselves from the pack. Others cope with life's losses by isolating themselves in a world of accomplishment to avoid future pain. As Simon and Garfunkel pointed out in song, a rock feels no pain, and an island never cries. Those with Type A behavior patterns are particularly prone to self-sufficiency as a way of life.[3]

"What do you really want out of life?" I cautiously asked a client one day.

The silence reverberated as he intimidated me with his piercing stare. I was routinely intimidated by Mike. His medical degree, wealthy lifestyle and indirect manner unsettled me. "I want to be successful," he finally said. "This month my practice is busier than it has ever been. I'll be billing a thousand dollars more than I ever have."

But his answer didn't satisfy me. It was much too shallow, given the time he had taken to formulate it. I felt that Mike's shallowness could be punctured with time.

"What's it all about?" I asked again several sessions later.

"I just want to be happy," he replied. "I just need more."

I kept asking, week after week, "What's it all about? What's the meaning of life?" Meanwhile his life got worse.

Emotional walls can be strong, but sometimes they crumble suddenly. One day, in response to the same question he had heard for weeks, Mike began to sob. "I don't know what it's all about. All my life I wanted to be somebody. I went to school because I thought a doctor was somebody. I always wanted a nice house with a Mercedes in the garage. Now I have them and they don't matter. Nothing really matters anymore."

Mike was trapped in a self-sufficiency loop. The more he searched for success, the more unsuccessful he felt. The more he searched for love, the more unloved he felt. At the core of his self-sufficiency was a lonely little boy who had never experienced unconditional acceptance. He kept repeating what he had learned to do as a child—trying to earn love through unusual accomplishment. His world of conspicuous consumption was carefully designed to earn approval, but it hadn't worked.

Mike wanted what most of us want. He wanted someone to love him unconditionally, to be faithful and devoted to him. But all his efforts to earn faithful love failed. Because we have been wounded by past relationships, we so easily slip into a *getting* mentality: "How can I find others who will be faithful to me and accept me unconditionally?" Like Mike, we try to *earn* unconditional love (notice the contradiction). Meanwhile, the most fulfilling, faithful relationships are experienced by those who are *giving* from the riches of faithful character.

Awareness Exercise

Did you recognize the common theme? In each of these implications, the question is changed from "Why are we faithful to one another?" to "Why are others faithful to me?" This subtle change makes a huge difference in how we view faithfulness. Rather than faithfulness being a part of our character, faithfulness is something we earn through conformity or success. Viewing faithfulness as a self-rewarding behavior inevitably causes us to think more about what we get than about what we give or who we are. Stress becomes the enemy because it interferes with our goals.

Faithfulness as Character Formation

Remember the friends I mentioned in chapter six, the ones who adopted five special-needs children? They refuse to view stress as their enemy and stress reduction as the best way to plan their future. As they navigate the challenges of parenting, they frequently remind themselves that God did not call them to be successful, only faithful. Faithfulness, to them, is not a set of behaviors designed to buy security or approval, but a way of life, a reflection of inner character.

In *Spirit Fruit,* John Drescher quotes Lienal Whiston: "The Christian is not called to be successful, but to be faithful. He [or she] is set free from the fear of failure or the compulsion to succeed."[4] Christianity calls us beyond self-centered views of faithfulness, self-sufficiency and approval, and invites us to learn from a faithful God.

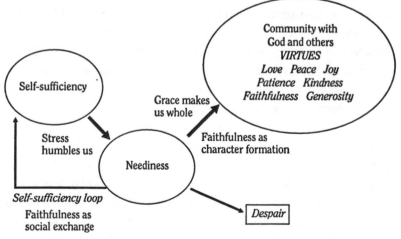

Figure 9

Faithful Character Is Formed Through Stress

Faithful character is not only tested through trials, it is actually formed through trials. James writes that trials *produce* endurance, maturity and completeness (James 1:2-4). Paul writes that suffering *produces* endurance, character and hope (Romans 5:3-5). It is not enough to survive stress by looking at it as a test of character. Stress defines and shapes and produces character. Although stress rarely makes us happy, it often produces fruit that nourishes the inner life.

When my oldest daughter was in third grade, she came home from school one day in despair. The other third-grade girls had banded together to form a "Cool Girls Club." Although Danielle had been invited by her closest friends, she declined because the club shut out other girls.

For several days Danielle went to school and came home with a poignant sadness on her face. For all she knew, she had lost her friends forever because she wasn't part of the club. Lisa and I felt Danielle's pain and wished we could do something to ease it, though we knew she had made the right decision. Fortunately, the club dispersed after a few days, and Danielle was reconciled with her friends.

Danielle is in high school now, and we often look back on that third-grade crisis as a formative event in her life. It's not just that those dreadful days *tested* her character, but they also *shaped* her character by helping Danielle define who she is and what she cares most about. She has many more stressors ahead, and each will help shape her character.

We normally assume that our actions are based solely on our attitudes and beliefs. Social psychologists tell us otherwise. Many times our attitudes follow upon our actions.[5] Danielle's decision to disagree with her friends forced her into a stressful and awkward position at school, and thereby strengthened her concerns for justice. Psychologist David Myers sums it up this way:

> The attitudes-follow-behavior principle has heartening implications. Although we cannot directly control all our feelings, we can influence them by altering our behavior. If we are unloving, we can become more loving by behaving as if we were so—by doing thoughtful acts, expressing affection, giving affirmation. . . . The moral: We can as easily act

ourselves into a way of thinking as think ourselves into a way of acting.[6] When we act faithfully in the face of trials, we strengthen our character and shape our will.

Faithful Character Is Formed Through Grace

Stress alone is not enough to make us faithful. Many individuals abandon important values in times of stress, while others strengthen their values through disciplined and virtuous behavior. What is the difference?

Those who act with virtue in the midst of stress and temptation are those who have seen faithfulness in others. A caring parent teaches a needy child about faithfulness by changing diapers and providing food and comfort. The child learns both roles—that of a needy child and that of a faithful caregiver.[7] When the child is grown, he or she is prepared to provide faithful care to others.

Similarly, when we are faithful to God, it is because God is first gracious and faithful to us. Jesus became like us, experienced every temptation and trial, and remained faithful.

> Therefore he had to become like his brothers and sisters in every respect, so that he might be a merciful and faithful high priest in the service of God, to make a sacrifice of atonement for the sins of the people. Because he himself was tested by what he suffered, he is able to help those who are being tested. (Hebrews 2:17-18)

Jesus' faithfulness was defined by his response to stress and temptation. Because he was faithful, and because of God's gracious gift of salvation, we grow in faithfulness through times of stress.

10

Gentleness

Gently, Lord, O gently lead us.
THOMAS HASTINGS

Your *spouse comes to you after several hours of brittle silence and* says, "I'm sorry. I know I shouldn't have spoken so harshly to you. It would have been wrong under any circumstances, but especially with your friends around. Will you forgive me?" How do you respond?

Jimmy didn't mean to hurt his little sister Annie. He just forgot she was so much smaller. He knew it was against the rules to push her, but he had no idea that she would fall back into that tree trunk and gash her head. After anxiously waiting for a call from the emergency room, he looks with frightened and tearful eyes as Dad and Mom walk in the door holding Annie's hands. He silently wonders, *Will they yell at me again? Will they ever forgive me?* How will Mom and Dad respond?

Melinda has worked behind the counter on her own for only two hours, and this is her first angry customer. She is quite sure she filled the order properly, but the red-faced man across from her insists that she shorted him a hamburger. What should Melinda do?

Your friend is helping you clean the kitchen when she drops your favorite bowl on the ceramic tile floor. She feels awful. So do you. How should you respond?

These are times for gentleness. Each situation illustrates the relationship between stress and gentleness. It's easy to be gentle when everything is going well. The children are in bed, you are sitting on the couch next to your favorite person. As you enjoy a warming fire while sipping a cup of espresso, you exchange gentle words. It's a beautiful picture, and it is easy to respond gently under these circumstances.

Gentleness as a virtue is defined in moments of stress more than moments of comfort. It's when the children are crying in bed, the one you love is out of town, the fire won't start because the kindling is too wet and the coffee is weak—that's when we need the inner virtue of gentleness to respond wisely.

Gentleness, like the other virtues we have considered, cannot be reduced to a set of behaviors. It is an inner state, a virtue that is forged in times of stress and revealed when others least expect it. The apostle Paul included the Greek word for gentleness among the fruits of the Spirit (Galatians 5:23), but most translators have preferred to render the word as "meek" rather than "gentle" because "gentleness" can too easily be reduced to a set of behaviors. Meekness is an inner quality, a way of approaching the world that transforms our emotions, thoughts and behaviors.

But *meekness* doesn't quite capture the Greek word Paul used. In our language we equate *meek* with *weak*, but that's not the word Paul used. Stephen Winward tells of an English soccer star, John Charles, who was known as "the gentle giant." Though Charles was strong and quick and agile, he played by the rules, never taking advantage of being behind the referee's back.[1] Moses was a strong and decisive leader, but he approached God with humility and reverence. Like John Charles, Moses was a meek man (Numbers 12:3) but not a weak man.

I use the word *gentleness* here because *meekness* is rarely used in today's parlance. But keep in mind that we are considering an inner quality of strength and not an outer façade of weakness and passivity.

Booker T. Washington knew about gentleness as a virtue. Born in 1856, he worked in coal mines as a child, taking off three months per year to go to school. His hard work paid off, and he graduated from Hampton Institute in 1875. Six years later he was appointed the first president of Tuskegee Institute, a trade school for African-Americans. After accepting the presidency, he was walking down an Alabama street one day when a white woman spotted him. Not recognizing who he was, she summoned him to come and chop some wood for her.

Most of us, in Washington's situation, would not have tolerated such racist treatment from the woman. We might have yelled, "Who do you think you are!" Or "You have oppressed my people long enough. No more!" Booker T. Washington had a different response. He took off his coat, chopped the wood and carried it into her house.

Later, when the woman discovered who he was, she came to his office to apologize. "It's all right," Washington said. "I delight in doing favors for my friends."[2] The woman became a very generous donor to Tuskegee Institute. And Washington went on to advise presidents Theodore Roosevelt and William Howard Taft as well as write several books.

I'm not sure if Washington's response to the woman was the only virtuous response, or even the best response. But one thing is sure—Washington knew that meekness is not weakness. He demonstrated strength through his gentle and kind responses to life's challenges. Jesus taught, "Blessed are the meek, for they will inherit the earth" (Matthew 5:5).

Of Course Not

Am I about to suggest that stress gives rise to gentleness? Does waiting in line at the grocery store make us more gentle with the checker? Does a flat tire on a family vacation make us more gentle with our loved ones? Does dieting make us easier to live with? Does a demanding and unreasonable boss make us gentler at work? Of course not. We are all vulnerable to negative effects of stress. However, moderate doses of stress help us empathize with those around us and can produce the inner character traits that allow us to remain gentle, even in times of stress.

One woman I discussed this book with described how she learned gentleness by walking with others through their times of pain. She sat by a dying friend during her final hours and walked through a long cancer treatment with another friend. Her conclusion? She has learned to embrace pain as God's tool for growth. "Pain tenderizes us and allows us to be more empathetic with others." Her conclusion is supported by stress research. Stress researcher Norma Haan found that empathy in adults is related to transitional life stresses in adolescence (for females) and early adulthood (for males).[3] Stress, in the proper dose and at the right time, builds our capacity for gently understanding and helping others.

This is not to say that gentleness is a natural response. It requires training, as do the other virtues—love, joy, peace, patience, kindness, generosity and faithfulness.

Many runners train at high altitudes where oxygen levels are sparse. If they discipline themselves to run under harsh circumstances, then they know they can succeed under normal circumstances. Runners are best trained at altitudes where no one wants to run, and gentleness is best trained in times of anger, when no one wants to be gentle.

Balancing Gentleness and Anger

Blessed with the gift of wisdom, Israel's king Solomon wrote, "A soft answer turns away wrath, but a harsh word stirs up anger" (Proverbs 15:1). Solomon captured the tension that exists between gentleness and anger. When Booker T. Washington chopped that woman's wood, wasn't he feeling rage inside? How could he respond so gently in the face of such obvious oppression and prejudice?

These are important questions we need to grapple with in training ourselves to be gentle. If we can learn to be gentle when we are angry, then we can be gentle at others times as well.

How would you respond to the situations described at the beginning of this chapter? Notice that in each case gentleness requires managing anger. Your spouse has just apologized, but you still feel the sting of embarrassment and anger. While your spouse is apologizing, your urge is to reply, "May the fleas of a thousand camels infest your armpits." But do you? Perhaps you go to the other extreme and say, "Oh, it's no big deal. I knew you didn't mean anything by it." Neither response is exactly appropriate in this situation.

Jimmy's parents face the same dilemma. They feel angry that he hurt his sister again. How many times will this happen before he learns to obey? The urge is to yell, but they know his deepest need is for tender mercy.

Melinda keeps telling herself that the customer is always right, but deep down she is enraged by this customer's audacity. How will she balance her rage and her desire to remain calm?

As your bowl drops to its death, you feel like performing your Bobby Knight imitation. It was your favorite bowl. But you care about your friend—you care enough to balance your anger with gentleness.

These are training opportunities—high-altitude exercises for those serious about learning gentleness. If we lean to the extremes of uncontrolled anger or suppressed anger, we do ourselves and others damage. A soft answer turns away wrath.

The Price of Uncontrolled Anger

Anger is a human emotion, and suppressing it causes problems. But when we lean too far toward embracing our anger, we also face difficulties. Have you ever wondered how much damage red-faced, angry basketball coaches do to themselves when they rant and rave about a bad call or a missed jump shot? Quite a lot. Those who are quick to react with hostility and anger are much more likely to have health problems and die by middle age than their gentle cohorts.[4]

Since the days of Aristotle we have heard about catharsis—the idea that venting anger is the best way to keep it from building up inside of us. Sigmund Freud thought catharsis helped his patients deal with rage and other feelings from their past. Therapists today accept the catharsis hypothesis when they give batacas (foam bats which are used to hit others without causing injury) to their clients and encourage them to let out their rage. Ann Landers once wrote that children should be taught to release their aggression on a punching bag or an old chair rather than people. Her advice got quite a response from one reader:

Dear Ann:

I was shocked at your advice to the mother whose 3-year-old had temper tantrums. You suggested that the child be taught to kick the furniture and "get the anger out of his system." I always though you were a little cuckoo. Now I'm sure.

My younger brother used to kick the furniture when he got mad. Mother called it "letting off steam." Well, he's 32 years old now and still kicking the furniture—what's left of it, that is. He is also kicking his wife, the cat, the kids, and anything else that gets in his way. Last October he threw the TV set out the window when his favorite team failed to score and lost the game. (The window was closed at the time.)

Why don't you tell that mother that children must be taught to control their anger? This is what separates civilized human beings from savages, Dummy.

Star Witness[5]

Was Ann Landers right when she advised her readers that children should be taught to vent their anger? Probably not. Was the respondent wise to express so much anger in response? Probably not. Under many circumstances, venting our anger only makes it stronger.[6]

Alfred Hitchcock went a step further, suggesting that watching violence on television keeps us from doing violent acts ourselves. "One of television's great contributions is that it brought murder back into the home where it belongs. Seeing a murder on television can be good therapy. It can help work off one's antagonisms."[7] But Hitchcock, like Freud, Aristotle and Ann Landers, is incorrect. Several decades of research suggest that viewing violence on television makes one more, not less, prone to aggression.

How often we read and hear advice to express our anger! "Get it off your chest. You have a right to express your feelings." How rarely we stop to think through the consequences of expressing our angry feelings. When we don't control our anger, we hurt ourselves and others.

The Price of Suppressed Anger

If we lean to the other extreme and hold in all feelings of anger, we do no better. Many centuries ago Buddha pronounced, "Anger will never disappear so long as thoughts of resentment are cherished in the mind." Just as those who are quick to anger are prone to heart problems, so are those who suppress their anger. Those who hold in their anger and nurse resentment are prone to high blood pressure and coronary heart disease.[8]

A relatively new area of stress research has to do with tension discharge rate (TDR). Those who hold in anger and harbor resentments have a slow TDR, and they pay a price for it. They have more health problems, more work absenteeism and worse job performance than those with rapid TDRs.[9]

Both extremes—hostile expression of anger and suppression and retention of anger—cause health and interpersonal problems. The key to managing anger is moderation: experience anger openly, express it cautiously and wisely, and refuse to let it linger. The apostle Paul instructed, "Be angry but do not sin; do not let the sun go down on your anger" (Ephesians 4:26). James wrote that we are to be "quick to listen, slow to speak, slow to anger; for your anger does not produce God's righteousness" (James 1:19-20). There are times when expressing anger is important, but maintaining gentleness is just as important.

The Essence of Gentleness

A virtuous response to anger begins in the inner life, before an outward response is ever made. Somewhere between uncontrolled expression of anger and suppressing anger, there is room for authentic gentleness and strength. It's not the intimidating strength of a screaming basketball coach, nor is it the passive power of a chronic victim. Rather, it is a virtuous strength expressed in kindness, directness and self-control. "One who is slow to anger is better than the mighty, and one whose temper is controlled than one who captures a city" (Proverbs 16:32). This is the strength that Booker T. Washington used to build a struggling trade school into a thriving institution. It is the strength that Mahatma Gandhi used to free the Indian people from oppression without resorting to violence. It is the strength of gentleness, defined in moments of stress.

The essence of gentleness is a capacity to value others as much as we value ourselves. Rage, with its intent to tear down others, has no place for the gentle. Neither does suppressing anger and nursing bitterness because to do so is to protect oneself by shielding another from truth. Gentleness means we care enough to tell the truth kindly.

Let's return once more to the example at the beginning of the chapter.

This situation presents a high-altitude training opportunity, a chance for gentleness, for valuing the other enough to tell the truth kindly.

Your spouse comes to you after several hours of brittle silence and says, "I'm sorry. I know I shouldn't have spoken so harshly to you. It would have been wrong to do under any circumstances, but especially with your friends around. Will you forgive me?" How will you respond?

This is an example of stress in action. During those hours of silence you may have rehearsed one hundred responses in your mind, but now it's time for a decision. Remember that gentleness is not just an action, but it flows out of our inner life. Those hours of rehearsal will make a difference in the response you choose.

Notice that power is the real issue here. Your spouse made a bad choice by criticizing you in public, putting you in a powerless position. Now you can drag your partner down with an aggressive or a passive response. You can gain more power by venting your anger, accusing your spouse of all sorts of disgusting things. Or you can gain more power by passively saying, "I'm getting used to it." Perhaps the silent treatment has served to punish and balance out the power. Remember though, those with slow tension discharge rates end up hurting themselves most.

The gentle response starts during those early minutes of silence. Remember, at the heart of gentleness is a capacity to value others as much as we value ourselves. Yes, you are feeling angry, but you also recall times when you have hurt your spouse. You contemplate how human fallenness affects every aspect of life—how many times others have responded graciously to you when you don't deserve kindness. You are training yourself in a moment of anger to be a more gentle person.

Finally you respond, "Yes, I forgive you. Thank you for apologizing. I brought it up because I felt really angry at the time. I'm still feeling some anger, but I'm remembering that I've hurt you before too, and these are the times we really need each other. I'm sorry for these hours of silence; it wasn't the right response on my part."

This gentle response is honest and strong, but kind and supportive at the same time. You are valuing your spouse as much as yourself—the key to gentleness.

A person I interviewed for this book described several major stressors: her mother's dying of a brain tumor, her brother's dying of AIDS, and her two children's health problems. After some years of reflection she was able to write, "The events of my life have allowed me to see and know God." She described how she is learning to be gentle by releasing her anger, her fears and her need to control. Stress is producing good fruit in her life.

Albert Thompson, a substitute teacher in Chicago, was accused of molesting ten fourth-grade children in 1994. He was immediately dismissed from his position, his name and picture were broadcast to homes throughout the nation, and the police department started a careful investigation. What they found was not what they expected. A nine-year-old child had paid nine classmates a dollar each to make up allegations of sexual abuse. A man's reputation was destroyed for nine dollars.

How did Thompson respond? With gentleness. Rather than expressing anger at the child welfare system that unfairly hurt him, he supported it, noting that children need protection from abusers. The rights of the children were as important to Albert Thompson as his own rights. This is the essence of gentleness. When talking with a *Chicago Sun-Times* reporter, Thompson quoted the Bible: "Weeping may endure for a night, but joy cometh in the morning." The reporter titled his article, "Faith Helped Teacher Deal with Charges."[10] Faith helps us deal with all kinds of stressors, just as it helped Albert Thompson.

A Context for Gentleness
Faith in a gracious God puts gentleness in context. Throughout Scripture we see the same rhythm we have discussed in this book: stress humbles us and grace makes us whole. The hassles and catastrophes of life remind us of our needy and humble position before our omniscient God. With time, repeated stress and enough failure, we get to a point where we allow God to touch us. David described his humble condition this way:

O LORD, my heart is not lifted up,
    my eyes are not raised too high;
I do not occupy myself with things
    too great and too marvelous for me.

But I have calmed and quieted my soul,
     like a weaned child with its mother;
my soul is like the weaned child
     that is with me. (Psalm 131:1-2)

The weeping that endures for a night is an essential part of becoming humble. Without weeping in the night, there is no joy in the morning.

From our position of neediness, God reaches down and finds us. We know God through Jesus Christ, who epitomized gentleness by valuing us enough to sacrifice himself for us, drawing us into community with God.

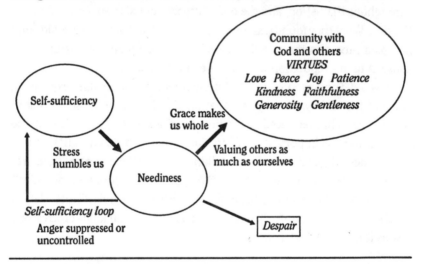

Figure 10

Jesus is the perfect model of gentleness: strong enough to drive out those who would turn the holy temple into a marketplace, compassionate enough to heal on the sabbath and humble enough to wash his disciples' feet. The gentleness of Jesus puts our quest for virtue in perspective:

Let the same mind be in you that was in Christ Jesus,
who, though he was in the form of God,
     did not regard equality with God
     as something to be exploited,
but emptied himself,
     taking the form of a slave,

being born in human likeness.
And being found in human form,
    he humbled himself
    and became obedient to the point of death—
    even death on a cross.
Therefore God also highly exalted him
    and gave him the name
    that is above every name,
so that at the name of Jesus
    every knee should bend,
    in heaven and on earth and under the earth,
and every tongue should confess
    that Jesus Christ is Lord,
    to the glory of God the Father. (Philippians 2:5-11)

If Jesus, the only human revelation of deity, humbled himself, then how else can we respond but to humble ourselves before God and one another? "Do nothing from selfish ambition or conceit, but in humility regard others as better than yourselves. Let each of you look not to your own interests, but to the interests of others" (Philippians 2:3-4).

This is what Booker T. Washington did when he chopped wood for his racist neighbor. Gentleness is not weak or passive. It is dynamic and powerful and would change the world if we really knew its power.

Facing the Enemy

Gentleness flourishes in a community where people are humbly aware of God's grace. Members of the first-century church sold their belongings, shared the profits, cared for the poor and lived in harmony with one another. They created what sociologists now call an intentional community. In the context of caring community, they developed "glad and generous" hearts together as they reflected daily on God's grace (Acts 2:44-47).

I'm not suggesting that Christians go back to a communal living situation (though some, like Jesus People USA, have done this), but we need to recognize the ideological enemy of community that lurks in every corner of American culture—individualism. We have been trained in this society to think of ourselves first and others second. We are convinced that our individual well-being is more important than the welfare of those around us. We are bombarded with messages like these:

☐ How could our economy survive without self-interest?

☐ Each person must vote for his or her own interests.

☐ I should love myself and think that I am wonderful!

A feature article in *Newsweek* described self-esteem as the latest national elixir.[11] Aren't we supposed to think of ourselves first? Anything else seems silly to us.

Of course there are benefits to positive self-esteem, but it seems that a reasonable concern for individual health has given way to an obsession with self-sufficiency. Those who excuse sin and fallenness as symptoms of poor self-esteem are only partly right, and they miss opportunities to humble themselves before a gracious God.

Individualism is also expressed in the way we define success—by dollars and titles, and not by service. In 1994, when Richard Herrnstein and Charles Murray published *The Bell Curve*,[12] a book arguing that IQ is the best predictor of success in American life, columnist Art Hilgart wrote a tongue-in-cheek column suggesting another possibility. Hilgart wrote that UQ (unscrupulousness quotient) is the best predictor of success in American life.[13] Those who break the rules and exploit others bring home the biggest paychecks. The article was clearly satirical, but it is amusing only because it seems partly true. Even more disturbing is the complete seriousness with which Herrnstein and Murray argued that IQ is the best predictor of success, without even questioning what success looks like. We are immersed in a society that values money more than virtue, and defines success accordingly.

This same individualism drives us toward pathologizing stress. We silently reason, *I don't like the way stress feels, and my job is to take care of myself, so stress must be bad and I ought to get rid of it.* We get caught in the self-sufficiency loop, feeling angry when we are inconvenienced and pressured when we have opportunities to serve others. The virtues discussed here—love, joy, peace, patience, kindness, generosity, faithfulness and gentleness—can be fully known only when we get beyond individualism and begin to care as much about others as ourselves.

Awareness Exercise

All of us, when we read chapters such as this, want to be more gentle with others. Try this approach:
1. Think of a person you are not naturally drawn to. Perhaps it is someone you are angry with—a competitive coworker, a former friend, an estranged family member.
2. Next, find one thing about this person that you like, and think about that good trait each time you remember the person.
3. Each time you are around the person, ask yourself what it would mean to care as much for this person as you care for yourself.

This exercise seems strange and foreign to us, doesn't it? We're not accustomed to loving our neighbors as ourselves. It's time we face the enemy of individualism and move on toward community.

Moving On

How do we move beyond the self-absorption that saturates American society? First, we must become critics of individualism and self-sufficiency. Just as millions of Americans are attached to one another on the information superhighway, so we are attached to one another socially. Psychologist and author James Lynch calls this connection a "social membrane." We are part of larger social organisms, and each of us suffers individual medical problems when we fail to recognize our part in this social network.[14] Not surprisingly, interpersonal conflicts are among the most damaging stressful events,[15] and healthy interpersonal relationships help people cope well with stress.[16] We need one another.

Second, we must challenge our views of stress as an obstacle to growth. Stress prepares us to experience the community around us, and to know the touch of a gracious and gentle God.

As with the other virtues, we can't just "put on" gentleness as an act of willpower. It takes training. Just as the committed runner trains at high altitudes, we train in moments of stress and anger. Stress prepares us to experience grace and develop qualities of gentleness. One of those I interviewed for this book came to an important conclusion after facing many months of significant stress: "I'm trusting God more. I can afford to be gentle."

11

Self-Control

He must increase, but I must decrease.
JOHN THE BAPTIST

Seven-month-old Brittany Stauss was sitting in a car seat in the back of her family's van when her father and another driver got involved in an angry exchange on a Chicago tollway. The shouting ended suddenly when the other driver pulled out a handgun and shot a bullet into the van and through Brittany's brain. This April 14, 1994, event sent reverberations throughout the nation, a symbol of concern among a people searching for values.

Brittany survived but may have permanent vision and hearing deficits.[1] Dr. John Ruge, Brittany's neurosurgeon, announced, "We can see where the bullet was. We can see the track it made. We can't see all the repercussions."

Similarly, most of us survive our impulse-driven society, although we are bombarded with events like this on the headline news, at the local video store and on prime-time television. But we, like Brittany, are left with deficits. Ours aren't as tangible as hers, but they shape the ways we see one another and often keep us from hearing God's calling. If we look carefully, we can see where damage is throughout our society and where self-control is missing. But we can't yet see all the repercussions.

We also see examples of those who have controlled themselves in the midst of trying circumstances. A. C. Green is an example. Several years ago members of the Portland Trailblazers basketball team were accused of sleeping with teenage girls on a road trip. The accusations were splashed across newspapers throughout the country. As the media investigated the claims, the sexual lifestyle of professional athletes became the subject of dinner conversations around the nation. Out of the smoldering remains of broken reputations and self-deceptive justifications, A. C. Green emerged with a different testimony. Green, an NBA star and committed Christian, promised God in 1981 that he would remain sexually abstinent until marriage. Even in the midst of a demanding NBA schedule, road trips and colleagues who tease him about his celibacy, he has remained faithful to God.[2]

How do we learn self-control in the midst of our human impulses and desires to eat too much, sleep too much (or with the wrong person), spend too much and shoot people on the tollway? That is, how do we manage this state of human fallenness that taints our thinking and feeling and desires? And how do we manage to be different in a society that scorns self-control? Stress, especially the stress of temptation, plays an important role.

Self-control requires willpower and fortitude, but even more important is the direction our heart leans in times of stress. Some respond to stress with humility and gentleness, working to manage temptation appropriately and looking beyond themselves for strength. They have discovered the secret of self-control. Others respond by frantically grasping, exerting power, trying to eliminate all temptation and looking within themselves for strength. They are looking for self-control in the wrong places.

Of Course Not

A simplistic understanding of this connection between stress, temptation and self-control can be devastating. Imagine a dieter deciding to go sit at a smorgasbord without eating, just to feel the stress of temptation. How successful would our dieter be? Or perhaps an alcoholic should go to a nightclub and sit at the bar, just to strengthen willpower. Or maybe everyone who struggles with sexual temptation should rent sexually explicit videos so they can learn to cope with temptation. Would this help? Of course not. It is silly to assume that walking into temptation will help us resist sin.

But many live at the other extreme, assuming the best Christians are those who are never tempted or at least never admit it. Imagine visiting a new church on a Sunday morning, without having prior experience with Christians. What would we see? We would observe devout, well-dressed people who talk about the joy of the Lord, their personal devotions and the essential role of Christian values in society. We would hear of their successes and the ways their values have led them to lives filled with peace and lasting love. As we walked out the door after the service, we would probably ache inside, feeling inadequate and empty, especially in comparison to this group of truly perfect people. Some might be attracted to this place and come back again. Others will conclude that church is only for perfect people, failing to recognize that every person in the church struggles with temptations— even those church members with a highly glossed exterior. By hiding and denying the temptations that haunt us, we Christians often leave one another feeling alone and isolated, and we end up struggling privately with issues better handled in the context of loving community.

When several researchers surveyed psychologists and asked how many of them have ever been sexually attracted to a client, 90 percent said they have been, at least on rare occasions.[3] When a colleague and I surveyed Christian counselors, using the same survey instrument, we found striking differences.[4] Whereas 90 percent of psychologists admit occasional sexual attraction to clients, only 58 percent of Christian counselors admit to such feelings. Is this good news or bad news? Do these survey results differ because many Christians have trained themselves to avoid sin by avoiding feelings of attraction, or because Christians have been socialized to deny temptation? As one involved in the ethics training of Christian psychologists, I must ask this question every semester. When I teach about ways to deal with sexual attraction toward clients, am I calling a problem into being or giving students tools to deal with the inevitable?

Here is another way to ask the same question: Does God build virtue in us by removing temptation or by giving us resources to cope with temptation? Let's test out each answer and see where it leads us.

Can We Avoid Temptation?

The first option is to assert that God builds character by removing temptation from our lives. In other words, virtuous Christians have learned to avoid temptation by making wise choices. This answer is partly right. Certain lifestyle choices make it easier to resist temptation. Just as the former alcoholic learns not to frequent taverns, the wise Christian learns to set careful standards regarding social activities, entertainment and interpersonal relationships. These standards shield us from unnecessary temptation and stress.

Virtuous people usually face fewer temptations. But we often turn this around and assume that those who face the fewest temptations are the most virtuous. This is not necessarily true. Consider the following logic problem.

Starting point: When A is true, then B is true. For example, when it snows, it is cold. For example, virtuous people face fewer temptations.

Turn it around: When B is true, then A is true. For example, when it is cold, it snows. For example, those with few temptations are virtuous.

What is true one direction is not necessarily true when it is turned around. Many times it doesn't snow when it is cold, and lack of temptation is not a good way to measure virtue. If it were, then what would we conclude about Jesus? Jesus faced many temptations and had perfect virtue.

Since, then, we have a great high priest who has passed through the heavens, Jesus, the Son of God, let us hold fast to our confession. For we do not have a high priest who is unable to sympathize with our weaknesses, but we have one who in every respect has been tested as we are, yet without sin. Let us therefore approach the throne of grace with boldness, so that we may receive mercy and find grace to help in time of need. (Hebrews 4:14-16)

So we come to the second possibility, that God builds our character by giving us resources to cope with the temptations we face. If this is true, as I have argued in this book, then we must concentrate on training ourselves to respond properly in the midst of stress and temptation.

Trials are an essential part of growth. The key is not *eliminating* temptation but *managing* temptation. Trying to eliminate temptation often makes it harder to manage, and managing temptation is often easier after shedding the unrealistic expectation that it can be eliminated.[5] Consider some examples.

☐ Sharon likes to shop. In fact, she likes to shop so much that her credit card balances are approaching their limits, and the family is facing financial problems.

☐ Mike likes the Internet. He spends hours searching for the latest image files of his favorite actresses, always hoping they won't be wearing many clothes.

☐ June likes to drink. She craves alcohol even when she wakes up in the morning and is starting to wonder if she has a drinking problem.

How successful will Sharon, Mike and June be if they try to eliminate temptation? Sharon could try to eliminate temptation by cutting up her credit cards. This may help her control her spending for a while. But will this really teach her to deal with the problem? There's always the checkbook—and remember cash? Until she learns to manage her spending, she won't experience self-control. What is it that she really longs for?

Mike might cancel his Internet subscription and try to eliminate his craving for fleshy photos. How successful will he be? Even at the supermarket he will be surrounded by quasi-pornographic images. His only hope is to find ways to manage the temptation. Mike can't escape sexual temptations in today's society.

June could search her house, throw away all alcohol and tell herself she will never drink again. Will these efforts to eliminate temptation help her a week from now when she is feeling stressed? Probably not. June needs to learn to manage her temptation. She can never eliminate it. Sharon, Mike and June need to admit their weaknesses and seek help from others.

When I Am Weak, I Am Strong

When Jimmy Swaggart's personal struggles became public in 1988, he faced his congregation in the midst of his shame and remorse and tried to explain. He knew what his followers were asking: "Why would our strong leader lead such a depraved secret sexual life?" Swaggart said he had asked himself the same question ten thousand times through ten thousand tears. His conclusion, in that painful sermon of confession, was that he had tried to live his entire life as if he were not human. He had tried to be strong through enormous willpower and determination, but it had not helped. As the apostle Paul said in Romans 7, the things he was doing were not the things he wanted to do, and the things he wanted to do were not the things he was doing. Fortunately, Paul found an answer (described in Romans 8) that depended on God's grace and not his own willpower.

Remember, self-control does not depend on willpower as much as it reflects the direction our heart leans in times of stress. When we try to eliminate temptation through the exercise of personal willpower, our problems deepen. When we humble ourselves and rest in the arms of a gracious God, we learn to manage temptation and experience greater self-control.

One of the biggest problems we face in self-control is getting beyond our belief that we can be strong. We so easily assume that willpower will get us through, and we long to be respected for our moral character and fortitude. When we fall down, we quickly get up and brush ourselves off, hoping no one else will see our weakness and vulnerability.

This desire for strength erodes quickly to image management. Even when we aren't strong, we feel a need to hide our weakness, to impress others despite our faults. We want to be respected for our moral character, our firm principles, our faithfulness, our resistance to temptation. But deep inside, we see our fragile neediness and brokenness. This creates a state of tension. For protection, we construct psychological armor, a glossy persona that we put on to convince others of our virtue and our strength. We can't admit our temptations because they make us look weak, so we try to eliminate or deny temptations rather than manage them. We must remain strong—after all, I'm OK, you're OK. Right?

No. It's not right. I'm fallen. You're fallen. Jimmy Swaggart is fallen. We are weak and needy people who like to pretend we are strong and capable. Sometimes we pretend pretty well and may even convince ourselves of our virtue and tenacity. But then stress and our stubborn independence drive us to our knees again, and we confront our neediness anew.

Millions of Americans have joined twelve-step groups because they realize their quest for power and independence has created problems and addictions in their lives. They come together in small groups and confess their weakness and neediness to one another. As they express their weakness, they find strength in community. One person I interviewed about this book said, "Self-control is an ongoing battle. Old habits die hard. That's where a twelve-step program helps me." The first step in these programs is to admit powerlessness—a difficult task in the midst of a society obsessed with power and strength.

Within the mental health field there is debate about the best way to help people. Some advocate teaching people greater power over their problems. Others favor teaching people to give up the frantic pursuit of control and power. One psychologist, Keith Humphreys, argues that psychotherapy points one direction whereas twelve-step programs lead in an entirely different direction.[6] According to Humphreys, twelve-step programs have the goal of self-abasement, while psychotherapy teaches self-enhancement. Two other psychologists, Robert Sollod and Marilyn Freimuth, assert that psychotherapy and twelve-step programs don't have to be as different as Humphreys implies, and that psychotherapists ought to question the individualistic assumptions of traditional psychotherapy.[7]

Twelve-step programs are not perfect. A partial understanding of the disease model of addictions often leads people to dismiss their responsibility in making choices. But their emphasis on admitting neediness is an essential step in healing, wholeness and self-control. Psychotherapy at its worst is done by self-deceived therapists who deny their own neediness and interdependence and try to convince others to do the same. At its best, psychotherapy is confessional. Hurting people express their neediness and brokenness, and a caring therapist is a minister of grace.

Many twelve-step programs have drifted from their Christian roots, and many forms of therapy point people toward a false confidence and autonomy. Neither is the perfect solution to human pain. But when done well, both reflect the rhythm that we see throughout Scripture: as we recognize our need, we turn to others and ultimately to God. The apostle Paul described his awareness of weakness and the strength he found in community with Christ:

If I must boast, I will boast of the things that show my weakness. . . .

Therefore, to keep me from being too elated, a thorn was given me in the flesh, a messenger of Satan to torment me, to keep me from being too elated. Three times I appealed to the Lord about this, that it would leave me, but he said to me, "My grace is sufficient for you, for power is made perfect in weakness." So, I will boast all the more gladly of my weaknesses, so that the power of Christ may dwell in me. Therefore I am content with weaknesses, insults, hardships, persecutions, and calamities for the sake of Christ; for whenever I am weak, then I am strong. (2 Corinthians 11:30; 12:7-10)

Weakness is not a noble goal in itself, but recognizing our inescapable weakness drives us toward others, and in many cases to Christ. As we train ourselves to be authentic with others about our weaknesses, remaining in relationship with Christ and others, self-control becomes a natural response of gratitude and faithfulness.

Awareness Exercise

Which direction does your heart lean in times of stress? Does it lean toward a quiet humility that allows you to draw close to others? Or does it lean toward stubborn independence that traps you in a self-sufficient loop?

Think about one temptation or struggle that has become a self-control battle for you. See which of the following fits your response best.

Humble awareness of neediness: I confess my struggle to a close friend, spouse, therapist or religious leader. I recognize my error and feel sorry for what I have done. I ask forgiveness from those I have hurt.

Stubborn independence: I get upset at myself and vow to never make the same mistake again. I feel shame and worry about someone finding out about me. I blame others who have hurt me in the past.

Self-control emerges from an accurate and humble awareness of human weakness. Stubborn independence brings shame, worry and neurotic efforts to maintain control. When we are weak, then we are strong.

John was a popular baptizer until Jesus started baptizing people on the other side of the Jordan River. Then everyone started going to Jesus. When John's followers came to him expressing concern, John didn't say, "Let's assert ourselves. We'll file a complaint with the chamber of commerce." No, his words were simple and clear: "He must increase, but I must decrease" (John 3:30). His heart was leaning the right direction.

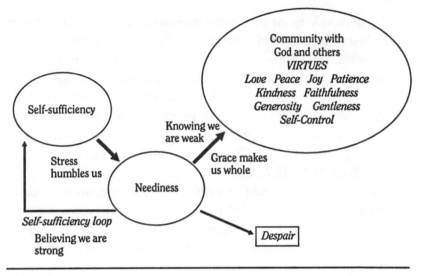

Figure 11

Postmodern Perils

My daughter decided she wanted to learn to juggle, so we found a juggling book and some beanbags for her birthday. Guess who ended up using them most? If you catch me on a good day, you may think I can juggle. But don't talk to me while I'm juggling, and don't make me laugh, because any little distraction will cause three beanbags to crash.

Learning to be authentic about our fallenness is like juggling in a hurricane. It's difficult enough to posture ourselves on our knees before God, but today's social climate makes it seem almost impossible at times. Scholars call today's prevailing social paradigm *postmodernism*. What is it, and how does it make self-control difficult? Let's take a brief historical survey, keeping in mind John's wise words: "He must increase, but I must decrease."

He Must Increase, but the Church Must Decrease

Our first stop on this historical survey is in the sixteenth century. At that time people looked to the church for authority. Rather than going directly to God, parishioners went to their priest who represented them to God and

God to them. This is similar to the corporate chain of command that is used in contemporary society. An employee with a concern is supposed to go to a direct supervisor rather than the chief executive officer. This system, when applied to spiritual life, created problems for the church in the Middle Ages. Martin Luther noticed that the sacramental system for receiving grace had lost its significance to many priests and parishioners, as they rushed through ceremonies without considering their religious meanings. The church had cashed in its power by selling indulgences (the message being "Pay the church this amount and your dead relative will be assured of life in heaven").

In 1517, on the day before All Saints' Day, Luther posted his ninety-five theses on indulgences on the Castle Church door. This action now symbolizes a revolution in religious thought.[8] Luther, John Calvin and other Reformers asserted that we can approach God directly. Grace is experienced personally through understanding God's character as revealed in Jesus Christ. The Reformers taught that Christ must increase, but the authority of the church, which had become a runaway train, must decrease.

I Must Increase, but He Must Decrease

That great event, the Reformation, changed the way many people view God. But all changes have ripple effects. As the Reformation empowered individuals, each individual's experience assumed importance. Two centuries later this new freedom evolved into the Enlightenment and then into modernism, intellectual movements that emphasized the power of individual knowing. Science and philosophy gained momentum, many countries became industrialized, and some believed that intellectual thought was destined to replace religion. Whereas science had to conform to religion in the Middle Ages, modernists believed that religion should conform to a rational, scientific understanding of the world.

Since Aristotle, the reasons for knowing had been (in order of importance) to discover truth, to act morally and to have power. Philosopher Peter Kreeft states that Francis Bacon (seventeenth-century Enlightenment philosopher) and modernity "have turned Aristotle upside-down."[9] Modernism, with its emphasis on knowing for the sake of power, has brought scientific, medical and industrial advances. It has also left many morally bankrupt and has reduced truth to what we can know through rational and natural methods.

Immanuel Kant and others argued that our views of God are inevitably bounded by human reason. This was the start of revisionist theology, which eventually reduced God's supernatural acts to metaphor or literary device rather than truth. It reduced Jesus to a good man rather than the God-man. Enlightenment ushered in a new view of Christ: "I must increase, but he must decrease."

I Must Increase, and You Can Do Whatever You Want

As devastating as modernism was to the moral fabric of Western society, the plot has thickened in recent years. As people have started questioning scientific and rational ways of knowing, we have moved into postmodernism, a paradigm that accepts multiple ways of knowing as equally valid.

We must be careful not to dismiss postmodern thinking altogether, because it has given a voice to diverse groups, including those who are oppressed. But postmodernism easily erodes to a sloppy relativism which asserts that all values are equally good and useful. One person understands the world through science. "That's fine," we say. Another person understands the world through mystical experiences. "To each his (or her) own," we conclude. Someone else finds meaning in orthodox religion. To this we say, "No problem; just don't try to convert others." We have come to a point where all meaning is constructed—if it means something to you, then it is important. Of course if this is true, then all meaning can also be deconstructed, and ultimately nothing is meaningful.

A 1994 *Newsweek* cover carried the headline "The Search for the Sacred: America's Quest for Spiritual Meaning."[10] The articles inside described our national exploration of New Age religion, Buddhism, Christianity and spiritism. Ironically, while we are searching for spiritual meaning, we are saying to one another that no one meaning is any more important than any other. If this is true, then nothing is ultimately meaningful apart from our subjective human experience. "I must increase, and you can do whatever you want."

No wonder it's hard to fall on our knees before God! Modernism taught us that religion is useful only if God does something for us—humans are the protagonists in this story. The Bible teaches us that God is the center of this world's story. Postmodern constructivism teaches us that God matters only if religion is important to us—that all of us write our own story. The Bible teaches us that we don't write very well, and that a more important story has already been composed. Relativism teaches us that we are strong, in control of our destinies, our beliefs, our values. The Bible teaches us that we are weak and needy. Humanism teaches us that our greatest hope lies in realizing our potential. The Bible teaches us that our greatest hope is in moving beyond ourselves and humbling ourselves before a gracious God. Pluralism teaches us that there are many ways to wholeness. The Bible teaches us only one way.

Practicing Weakness

The messages of relativistic postmodern thinking surround us in contemporary culture: Express yourself! Be your own person! Stand up for your rights! These messages are like my daughter's first experience with hairspray—they aren't all bad, but they have been overapplied.

Expressing ourselves and standing up for our rights can be a good thing. Our governmental system, for example, is based on the assumption that those who are concerned about a problem will express themselves. We need to speak out for justice in society. Similarly, our awareness of minority groups has been enhanced by people's speaking out. People experiencing oppressive situations need to be empowered to speak up about injustice. Women have made significant advances because they expressed themselves. People of color are doing the same. Abused spouses need to be empowered to escape life-threatening relationships.

It's not a bad message, but it is overapplied. Sometimes we get so accustomed to expressing ourselves that we assume we are right and others ought to conform to our views. We put ourselves in the center of power and confuse power with truth. In generations past we looked outside ourselves for truth—to the Bible or the church or a monarch. Today we look inside ourselves. Premodern thinkers might have said, "It's true because the church says it is true." Modern thinkers say, "It's true because it is rational and can be scientifically proved." Postmodern thinkers say, "It's true because I believe it is true." In other words, "I'm happy, and that's all that matters." Maybe that's not all that matters.

If we believe we find truth within ourselves, then our heart leans the wrong way when stressed—toward control and grasping ambition. When we feel stress, we assume it must be because we are not expressing enough control over the world around us. So we grasp at people and things more tightly than ever. Stress makes us more determined to express ourselves and less inclined toward virtue.

An elderly psychologist once told me that she had noticed a dramatic increase in marital problems with the rise of postmodernism. When partners accepted the assumption that expressing themselves was the most important thing, their marriages started falling apart. When husbands and wives stopped trying to control their anger and jealousy and fear, and started expressing and justifying their feelings, their closest relationship felt the strain. There must be a better way.

While worshiping in a Quaker church, I learned about what Quakers call queries. These are questions they ask themselves regularly to assess their values and perspectives. I have developed my own queries which I have used over the past couple of years to help me resist the trend toward grasping ambition I see all around. Here are my queries:

1. Do I live out my values in my relationships at home, work and school? Am I spending time with my spouse and children? Do I listen intently when they speak to me? When those closest to me need encouragement, am I available to them?

2. Are my behaviors consistent with my understanding of God's will? Do I value authenticity and honesty above success? Do I value compassion more than accumulating possessions? Do I allow my theological views to escape church and classroom boundaries and saturate my life so that I can be a living sacrifice to God?

3. Am I still motivated by ministry goals? Do I long to help those in need, pointing them toward greater awareness of God, others and self? Do I adhere to ethical standards for the sake of others and not just for personal protection?

4. Do I care for myself by exercising regularly, eating well, socializing frequently and thinking critically? Do I take time to enjoy beauty in God's creation?

5. Are my times of spiritual renewal regularly and freely chosen? Do I converse with God throughout the day? Am I responding to God's grace rather than trying to earn God's love? Do I work to identify and change problem areas in my life?

6. Are my words to others forthright and kind? Am I saying no to some things so I can say yes to others? Are others aware of my opinions on important matters?

7. Am I willing to sacrifice financial security for something challenging? Do I think more about what I am doing this week than about what I will do next year, ten years from now or when I retire?

8. Do I look forward to each new day? Am I engaged in the lifelong process of learning? Do I read regularly and discuss ideas with others frequently? Am I open to new experiences?

9. Do I use my time productively and efficiently? Am I planning ahead and pacing my work? Am I infusing energy and creativity in the things I research and looking for fresh ways of presenting my ideas?

The messages of postmodernism bend us toward self-sufficiency, and I'm sure some of my queries are tainted by these social trends. Self-control and, I hope, most of these queries require us to lean the other way. James tells us to humble ourselves before the Lord (James 4:10). Paul instructs us to be subject to one another out of reverence for Christ (Ephesians 5:21), to outdo one another in showing honor (Romans 12:10) and to regard others as better than ourselves (Philippians 2:3). These are not the messages of postmodernism.

Awareness Exercise

Try developing your own set of queries. Feel free to borrow from my list, but customize yours to the specific challenges you face.

Some go to a different extreme and become self-deprecating. They seem to believe that they must decrease and everyone else must have power over them. Self-deprecation is not the goal of virtuous living. In fact, self-deprecation leads people to the same problem as self-sufficiency. Both the one who thinks he is great and the one who thinks she is terrible end up thinking about themselves most of the time. Both remain in a state of self-absorption.

We've all seen people engaged in enthusiastic hugging. They lean into each other and accept support from each other. We've also seen people embrace cautiously, leaning away from one another to avoid closeness. When we think too little of ourselves or too much of ourselves, we lean away from God and others. Practicing weakness requires us to lean into others, to admit our needs and human weaknesses, many of which are shared with all other humans, and to look for strength in someone greater. The message of self-control is that we must decrease and *Christ* must increase. Self-control is found in community with God and others.

Awareness Exercise

Do you have a nagging problem that you can't seem to bring under control? Try this. Tell your problem to God and one other person. Make sure you choose someone who will keep your problem confidential. If you don't have a spouse or friend you can trust to keep it quiet, then seek out a pastor or a therapist.

It's hard to discuss problems with others, but once you do, you may find you have unlocked yourself from the power of your problem and that it no longer has the same grip on your life. Confession is an essential part of self-control. This will work best if you regularly discuss your struggles and temptations with God and one other person.

Stress tests our commitment to community and gives us opportunity to reach out to God and others in times of need. Jesus spoke these rather puzzling words:

> Come to me, all you that are weary and are carrying heavy burdens, and I will give you rest. Take my yoke upon you, and learn from me; for I am gentle and humble in heart, and you will find rest for your souls. For my yoke is easy, and my burden is light. (Matthew 11:28-30)

Sometimes life doesn't feel so easy, and our burdens don't feel so light. Jesus is saying, "Stop trying to do it on your own. Lean in to me." As we lean our hearts toward humility, toward recognizing our weakness, we find strength in community with Christ and others who know Christ.

12

Stress & Redemption

What was dull becomes sharpened,
what was crooked becomes straight,
what was weak becomes strong,
and what was useless becomes valuable.
MAX LUCADO

A *long the back roads that divide farmland in western Oregon's* Willamette Valley, I have noticed something peculiar. At virtually every intersection is a sign pointing to Woodburn, a rural community between Portland and Salem. This works out well for those driving to Woodburn. If they get lost, they just wait until the next intersection. Those who aren't headed for Woodburn often end up there anyway! It seems all signs point to Woodburn.

All creation points to redemption. We know this intuitively but rarely verbalize it. We see it in the big problems that surround us. How do we respond to news reports about the latest gang murders and child molestations? We say something is terribly wrong and needs to be changed. When sickness strikes a family member, we long for an eternity where sickness is obsolete. Families are torn apart by alcoholism, divorce and unfaithfulness. Our world, and everyone in it, is broken and in need of help.

The little problems of life also point to our need for redemption. Any one of life's hassles isn't so bad, but the hassles add up, and our needs become obvious. What do we say when we are stuck on a crowded freeway? We conclude that the road system is flawed and needs to be improved. When our bodies start bulging and sagging, we talk about our need for exercise or dieting. The roof starts leaking, the car runs rough, the dishwasher makes a funny noise, the family dog dies, the alarm clock doesn't work, the stereo blows a fuse, the upholstery on the new couch starts wearing thin, the floors need refinishing. We feel overwhelmed with the state of our broken, fallen world. Everywhere, we are surrounded by our need.

Three decades of self-help have been telling us that we can manage our stress and lunge ahead with our self-sufficient lifestyles. But our denial is wearing thin. Even after organizing our time and managing our stress, our lives and our world are still broken down and need repair. Every road we choose points to our need for our gracious God.

The Author of Stress
In the beginning, or shortly after the beginning, God created stress. God's first human creatures enjoyed bounty and peace and community. Then sin entered the world through their rebellion. When God cursed Adam and Eve for their deliberate choice to sin, was it a curse of punishment? Yes, in one sense. But even that punishment pointed toward redemption. Rather than allowing Adam and Eve to stay in the Garden and eat from the tree of life, which would have destined them to wallow in sin forever, God sent them out. He gave them stress and death, and ultimately redeemed humankind by showing us our desperate need for God.

Stress was not invented by industrialized society. Sure, industrialization has worsened the problem through long work weeks, unrealistic expectations, competitiveness and technology. But people have always been plagued by stress and have always suffered sickness and pain because of stress. God created stress to remind us of our neediness. This is a familiar concept: all around us we find reminders of need. The fuel indicator reminds us to stop for gas soon, the beeping timer on the oven reminds us to remove the casserole, the scales remind us to buy low-fat yogurt, speed limit signs remind us that we need to control our vehicles, drowsiness in church reminds us we need to go to bed earlier on Saturday night. Stress reminds us we have needs—physical needs, emotional needs and deep spiritual needs—for community with God.

Stress Is Necessary but Not Good

Of course we must be careful not to glamorize stress or trials. When we do, our natural response to others is to be trite or superficial in the midst of their pain. I doubt Adam and Eve skipped out of the Garden saying, "Oh boy, we now have the gift of stress! We get to fight thorns and agonize in childbirth!" No, they were undoubtedly sad and broken, and their years of stress added to their sadness.

Stress is not good. It taxes our immune systems, makes us vulnerable to sickness, contributes to irritability, keeps us awake at night and erodes our confidence. Stress brings headaches, sweaty hands, erratic breathing, back pain, muscle tremors, arthritis, acne, allergies, skin rashes, appetite changes and even dandruff.[1] And stress drives many to despair, resulting in soaring suicide rates, widespread clinical depression, crimes of desperation and interpersonal tragedies. Stress is not good.

But is stress really the "wild beast facing modern man," as one insurance brochure claims?[2] Is stress itself the enemy, or is stress a reminder of the enemy? Our answer to this question will determine our response to stress. Let's consider the two options.

Stress as the Wild Beast

The most prevalent answer to the question is that stress is our enemy. We are told that stress management will free us to live enjoyable, productive lives. Consider the following example.

Frank is an advertising executive who sees a counselor for stress-related problems at the request of his physician. His job is demanding, requiring sixty to seventy hours each week, his marital relationship is failing, and his adolescent children are rebelling. Frank suffers stress-related symptoms such as headache, insomnia, weight gain and irritability. Three months on an antidepressant has not helped much.

The counselor listens to Frank's story and teaches him stress management skills. Frank learns progressive relaxation to help him through each day. He also learns to talk to himself in calming ways: *I'm a good person even if my family members don't appreciate me. If my marriage doesn't work out, I can find happiness in other ways. I'm a successful executive. If my company doesn't value my work, I can always find a better position.*

With time, Frank feels better and stops seeing the counselor. He seems a little nicer at home, and his family relationships improve a bit. Everyone feels good about the treatment he received.

In one sense, this is adequate mental health treatment which frees Frank for a better life. But it doesn't address his inner experience of loneliness and pain. Sure, he has some tools to supercharge his self-image and push ahead in life for another year or two, but sometimes he still lies awake at night and wonders where life is pointing. After a while, he figures he'd better go back to his doctor and get some more pills or assertiveness training because he is starting to feel stressed again.

If stress is the enemy, then it is unnecessary and ought to be eliminated. But we are forever frustrated with this goal. Nothing we try takes away our stress. It haunts us until we die.

Stress as a Reminder of the Wild Beast

Another approach is to see stress not as our enemy, but as a reminder of our enemy. Stress points us to our weaknesses. Stress itself is not the wild beast. It is a reflection of the real beast—human fallenness and sin. This doesn't mean all stress results from personal sin. The roof doesn't leak because the homeowner yelled at the kids. Traffic isn't slow as a punishment for someone who flirted with a coworker that day. We don't lose our keys because we have broken the speed limit. Stress doesn't always reflect personal sin, but all stress reflects human fallenness.

Our fallenness affects our parenting, even as it affected our parent's parenting. So our children grow up with emotional scars, as we did. Sin affects our relationships, so we are hurt by some and we hurt others. Sin affects our perceptions, so we see things through the filter of our self-serving biases, assuming things ought to go the way we want them to. Sin affects the economy, shaping the way we view our work, our shopping and our taxes. Sin affects the environment, so we struggle with pollution and toxicity.

We are not merely victims of stress. We are participants, creators, evokers of stress. Everything around us points to our need for redemption from a world permeated by human fallenness.

What if Frank sees a counselor who has a different approach?

The counselor listens to Frank's story and helps Frank explore his deepest fears and assumptions. Over a period of several months, Frank gains insight into his feelings of inadequacy and loneliness. He realizes that his long work weeks, his unrealistic demands on family members and his hard-driving competitiveness all stem from his underlying assumption that others will love and accept him only if he is perfect.

Over time Frank learns to relax his perfectionistic demands and reduce his work hours and begins to recognize his faults and weaknesses. He becomes more vulnerable and tender in his relationships and finds people more accepting and loving. As he recognizes his weaknesses, Frank draws closer to others.

If stress is not the enemy but points us toward our weakness, then our goal is not to eliminate stress but to manage it by establishing self-awareness and virtue in the context of healthy relationships. Stress will always be with us, reminding us of our need, pushing us beyond our shallow self-sufficiency, pointing us to One greater than ourselves. Stress is not intrinsically good, but it is a necessary part of understanding our neediness before God and others. Stress points us toward redemption.

Stressed and Blessed?

We all have beliefs and values that shape our views of the world. These beliefs and values are created, in part, by the society that surrounds us. Today most people value happiness more than truth. Philosopher Peter Kreeft writes, "The typically modern mind is much more subjectivistic than the premodern mind. It seeks happiness rather than blessedness, feeling rather than fact."[3]

The social forces of modernism and postmodernism affect us in ways we seldom question. Many comfort themselves with the postmodern adage "If you're happy, that's what really matters." Few question the validity of the adage. Because the subtle relativism of postmodernism surrounds us, most of us have a belief like this one lurking within our psyche: *I ought to be happy, and stress interferes with happiness, so I ought to avoid stress.*

We have confused happiness with blessedness. Rather than longing for the virtuous character that comes from God's blessings, we strive for temporary happiness. As a result, what are the things that we find the most appealing and compelling? Super-size fries, new-release videos, pay raises, promotions, Super Nintendo games, cellular phones, alcohol, television, drugs, Dolby surround sound, sex, new clothes, the Internet and roller coasters. If it feels good, do it! Just do it! Whatever turns you on! Life is short; play hard!

Kreeft asserts that the crucial distinction between happiness and blessedness is suffering. Suffering can be part of blessedness, but it can never be part of happiness. When we value happiness more than blessedness, we don't tolerate suffering, so it shouldn't surprise us that skills to avoid, manage and limit stress are highly valued today.

Thriving in the midst of stress requires us to trade in our worship of happiness and our postmodern beliefs about stress for an older model: *I want to be blessed with virtuous character, and God shapes my character through trials and the community of truth.*

With this belief we value virtue more than pleasure, blessedness more than happiness. Throughout Scripture we see virtue valued above happiness and stress reduction. Think of the vivid characters in Scripture. How would their lives have been compromised if they had avoided stress in order to pursue happiness? Abraham could have enjoyed his wealth in Ur rather than searching the desert for the Promised Land. Moses could have remained a rich heir of Pharaoh rather than leading a half million slaves. Esther could have played it safe in the harem rather than risking her life to approach the king. David could have quailed before Saul's power and gone back to a tranquil life of shepherding. The prophets could have decided silence is golden. The apostles could have returned to fishing. Paul could have settled into a successful career as a journeyman tent maker. After considering a similar list, the author of Hebrews had this to say about the most faithful of all Bible characters:

Therefore, since we are surrounded by so great a cloud of witnesses, let us also lay aside every weight and the sin that clings so closely, and let us run with perseverance the race that is set before us, looking to Jesus the pioneer and perfecter of our faith, who for the sake of the joy that was set before him endured the cross, disregarding its shame, and has taken his seat at the right hand of the throne of God. (Hebrews 12:1-2) Jesus anchored the scale on life stress—homeless, ridiculed, abused, abandoned, stripped, mocked, crucified. We might all read the Bible more if it instructed us to be happy. But it doesn't. Scripture teaches us to be faithful, set apart for God's service. In the process we struggle with sin, bump into our brokenness over and over, and are led into a healing and redemptive relationship with our gracious God. Stress is part of the process.

We can be stressed and blessed at the same time. Those who shared their stories with me as I prepared to write this book consistently emphasized how stress had helped shape their character. Chronic illnesses, broken relationships, major job changes and personal losses produced a capacity for love, joy, peace, patience, kindness, generosity, faithfulness, gentleness and self-control.

One wise respondent, widowed in midlife when her husband died in a tragic accident, told me that the best stress management tool is found in understanding the purpose of stress. When we see stress as God's tool for shaping our character, we can cope, and even thrive, in the midst of stress. When we see stress as our enemy, we are easily overwhelmed.

Another respondent shared his belief that we cannot grow as Christians without stress. Another said that he has learned to be a producer of the fruit of the Spirit, and not just a consumer. Those who cope well with stress are able to see value in their painful experiences.

A Fruit Basket

Unlike an apple tree, which produces the same type of fruit every year, stress produces many types of fruit. We have considered love, joy, peace, patience, kindness, generosity, faithfulness, gentleness and self-control in separate chapters, but these fruit cannot actually be separated. They come in the basket of assorted fruit that we think of as virtuous character.

Healthy love, for example, makes us more patient with the people in our lives. As we are patient, we are able to express more kindness and exert more control over angry impulses. We experience more joy as our relationships become healthier. The virtues are related, as if in a big circle, with each strengthening the others. Each time we learn about kindness, we also learn about faithfulness and gentleness. Each time we refrain from a critical word, we learn both self-control and kindness. The virtues can be separated for the sake of discussion only. In real life, they are intermingled.

Christ does not call us to a virtue-of-the-month club. We cannot simply add to our patience one month, our joy the next, our love the following and so on. Christ calls us to transformed character. The more we understand God, and the deeper we enter into the spiritual life through the transforming power of Christ, we cannot help but be changed. The more we are changed, the more we recognize the inseparable nature of the fruit of the Spirit. The apostle Paul wrote to the faithful saints at Philippi: "I am confident of this, that the one who began a good work among you will bring it to completion by the day of Jesus Christ" (Philippians 1:6). Christ is the one who does the work and deserves credit for the fruit in our lives. Human virtues are only a dim reflection of the character of God.

Moving Forward

Roy Riegels had the right intention when he recovered a Georgia Tech fumble in the 1929 Rose Bowl game. His University of California teammates were no doubt delighted—at first. But in the midst of the emotion and confusion of the day, Roy started running toward his own goal line. Just before he reached the end zone, one of his own teammates tackled him. Roy had the right idea but went the wrong way with it.

How often do we do the same thing Roy Riegels did? We see stress before us, and then we start running the wrong way. It's time for someone to tackle us, grab us by the shoulders, look straight in our eyes and get us moving the right direction. Stress isn't a bad thing that should always be avoided; it can be God's tool to shape our character. Author Max Lucado writes this about times of stress:

> To melt down the old and recast it as new is a disrupting process. Yet the metal remains on the anvil, allowing the toolmaker to remove the scars, repair the cracks, refill the voids, and purge the impurities. And with time, a change occurs: What was dull becomes sharpened, what was

crooked becomes straight, what was weak becomes strong, and what was useless becomes valuable.[4]

Stress helps us understand our need for God. It allows us to understand our weakness so we can know God's strength.

This theology of redemption is very practical—it comes to life in those who are honest about their need. Sadly, many scurry around trying to pretend they don't need to be redeemed. Others get caught up in their stress and don't think to look beyond themselves for hope.

Once we move beyond the myths of self-sufficiency and the compelling desire to see ourselves as victims, our need for redemption is seen in our deep emotional longings. Underneath the anger and the fear is a profound human loneliness that only the most courageous and the most broken are willing to see. We long for community, for closeness, for someone to listen without giving advice, for an unconditional embrace. All creation, including our stress and loneliness, points us toward redemption.

Notes

Chapter 1: The Big Squeeze

[1]L. Harris, *Inside America* (New York: Random House, 1987).

[2]Richard Lazarus, "Little Hassles Can Be Hazardous to Health," *Psychology Today* (July 1981): 58-62.

[3]Ross Norman, "When What Is Said Is Important: A Comparison of Expert and Attractive Sources," *Journal of Experimental Social Psychology* 12 (1976): 294-300.

[4]Stephen G. West and T. Jan Brown, "Physical Attractiveness, the Severity of the Emergency and Helping: A Field Experiment and Interpersonal Simulation," *Journal of Experimental Social Psychology* 11 (1975): 531-38.

[5]Kenneth Dion, Ellen Berscheid and Elaine Walster, "What Is Beautiful Is Good," *Journal of Personality and Social Psychology* 24 (1972): 285-90.

[6]R. D. Elliott and D. H. Shamblin, *Society in Transition* (Englewood Cliffs, N.J.: Prentice-Hall, 1992).

[7]Nijole V. Benokraitis, *Marriages and Families* (Englewood Cliffs, N.J.: Prentice-Hall, 1993).

[8]National Center for Health Statistics, cited in David G. Myers, *Psychology*, 3rd ed. (New York: Worth, 1992).

[9]Rena R. Wing and Robert W. Jeffrey, "Outpatient Treatments of Obesity: A Comparison of Methodology and Clinical Results," *International Journal of Obesity* 3 (1979): 261-79.

[10]Sheldon Cohen, "Psychosocial Models of the Role of Social Support in the Etiology of Physical Disease," *Health Psychology* 7 (1988): 269-97.

[11]Anita DeLongis, Susan Folkman and Richard S. Lazarus, "The Impact of Daily Stress on Health and Mood: Psychological and Social Resources as Mediators," *Journal of Personality and Social Psychology* 54 (1988): 486-95.

Chapter 2: Stress Management

[1]Robert Mearns Yerkes and J. D. Dodson, "The Relation of Strength of Stimulus to Rapidity of Habit-Formation," *Journal of Comparative and Neurological Psychol-*

ogy 18 (1908): 459-82.
[2]Cited by A. Keister, "The Uses of Anger," *Psychology Today* 26 (July 1984).
[3]Hans Selye, "A Syndrome Produced by Diverse Nocuous Agents," *Nature* 138 (1936): 32.
[4]Robert Cialdini, *Influence* (New York: William Morrow, 1984), p. 28.
[5]For a review, see Mark W. Lipsey and B. David Wilson, "The Efficacy of Psychological, Educational and Behavioral Treatment," *American Psychologist* 48 (1993): 1181-209.
[6]Johann M. Stoyva and John G. Carlson in *Handbook of Stress: Theoretical and Clinical Aspects,* ed. Leo Goldberger and Shlomo Breznitz, 2nd ed. (New York: Free Press, 1993), pp. 724-56; Charles R. Carlson and Rick H. Hoyle, "Efficacy of Abbreviated Progressive Muscle Relaxation Training: A Quantitative Review of Behavioral Medicine Research," *Journal of Consulting and Clinical Psychology* 61 (1993): 1059-67.
[7]E. Stark, "Stress: It's All Relative . . . and Relatively Easy to Manage," *American Health,* December 1992, pp. 41-42, 44-47.
[8]Thomas H. Holmes and R. H. Rahe, "The Social Readjustment Rating Scale," *Journal of Psychosomatic Research* 11 (1967): 213-18.
[9]Suzanne C. Kobasa, "Stressful Life Events, Personality and Health: An Inquiry into Hardiness," *Journal of Personality and Social Psychology* 37 (1979): 1-11.
[10]Kenneth D. Allred and Timothy W. Smith, "The Hardy Personality: Cognitive and Physiological Responses to Evaluative Threat," *Journal of Personality and Social Psychology* 56 (1989): 257-66.
[11]*Newsweek,* June 13, 1994, pp. 31-39.
[12]Peter Kreeft, *Back to Virtue: Traditional Moral Wisdom for Modern Moral Confusion* (San Francisco: Ignatius, 1992).

Chapter 3: Love

[1]April O'Connell, Jacqueline Whitmore and Vincent O'Connell, *Choice and Change: The Psychology of Adjustment, Growth and Creativity,* 2nd ed. (Englewood Cliffs, N.J.: Prentice-Hall, 1985), p. 296.
[2]Peter Kreeft, *Back to Virtue: Traditional Moral Wisdom for Modern Moral Confusion* (San Francisco: Ignatius, 1992), p. 76.
[3]David Friend and editors of *Life* magazine, *The Meaning of Life* (Boston: Little, Brown, 1991), pp. 107, 118, 121, 152.
[4]J. A. Lee, "Love-Styles," in *The Psychology of Love,* ed. Robert J. Sternberg and Michael L. Barnes (New Haven, Conn.: Yale University Press, 1988), pp. 38-67.
[5]B. Livermore, "The Lessons of Love," *Psychology Today,* March/April 1993, pp. 30-34, 36-39, 80.
[6]I. Lisa McCann, David K. Sakheim and Daniel J. Abrahamson, "Trauma and Victimization: A Model of Psychological Adaptation," *Counseling Psychologist* 16 (1988): 531-94.
[7]C. S. Lewis, *The Four Loves* (New York: Harcourt, Brace and World, 1960).
[8]Livermore, "Lessons of Love."

[9]Kenneth S. Pope and Jacqueline C. Bouhoutsos, *Sexual Intimacy Between Therapists and Patients* (New York: Praeger, 1986).

[10]Abraham H. Maslow, *Motivation and Personality* (New York: Harper, 1954).

[11]Lewis, *Four Loves,* p. 12.

[12]Robert Bly, *Iron John: A Book About Men* (New York: Vintage, 1990), p. ix.

[13]Stuart Miller describes his lifelong search for male friendship and the many obstacles he faced—obstacles men construct in order to keep a "safe" distance from one another—in *Men and Friendship* (San Leandro, Calif.: Gateway, 1983).

[14]Herb Goldberg, *The Hazards of Being Male* (New York: New American Library, 1976).

[15]Hans Selye, "History of the Stress Concept," in *Handbook of Stress: Theoretical and Clinical Aspects,* ed. L. Goldberger and S. Breznitz, 2nd ed. (New York: Free Press, 1993), pp. 7-17.

[16]Joseph Mehr, *Abnormal Psychology* (New York: Holt, Rinehart and Winston, 1983), p. 11.

Chapter 4: Joy

[1]David Friend and editors of *Life* magazine, *The Meaning of Life* (Boston: Little, Brown, 1991), p. 187.

[2]William G. Morrice, *Joy in the New Testament* (Greenwood, S.C.: Attic, 1984).

[3]Stephen F. Winward, *Fruit of the Spirit* (Grand Rapids, Mich.: Eerdmans, 1981).

[4]Gerald F. Hawthorne, *Philippians* (Waco, Tex.: Word, 1987).

[5]John Bowlby, *Attachment and Loss,* vol. 1 (New York: Basic Books, 1969).

[6]Abraham H. Maslow, *Motivation and Personality,* 2nd ed. (New York: Harper & Row, 1970).

[7]A fuller account of this anecdote is found in John M. Drescher, *Spirit Fruit* (Scottdale, Penn.: Herald, 1974), p. 85.

[8]Donald Postema, *Space for God: The Study and Practice of Prayer and Spirituality* (Grand Rapids, Mich.: CRC Publications, 1983).

[9]Mark R. McMinn, *Cognitive Therapy Techniques in Christian Counseling* (Waco, Tex.: Word, 1991).

[10]C. S. Lewis, *Surprised by Joy* (New York: Harcourt, Brace and World, 1955).

Chapter 5: Peace

[1]Stephen F. Winward, *Fruit of the Spirit* (Grand Rapids, Mich.: Eerdmans, 1981).

[2]Paul R. Yarnold and Laurence G. Grimm, "Time Urgency Among Coronary-Prone Individuals," *Journal of Abnormal Psychology* 91 (1982): 175-77.

[3]Meyer Friedman and Ray H. Rosenman, "Association of Specific Overt Behavior Pattern with Blood and Cardiovascular Findings," *Journal of the American Medical Association* 169 (1959): 1286-96; C. David Jenkins, Stephen J. Zyzanski and Ray H. Rosenman, "Risk of New Myocardial Infarction in Middle-Aged Men with Manifest Coronary Heart Disease," *Circulation* 53 (1976): 342-47; Ray H. Rosenman et al., "Coronary Heart Disease in the Western Collaborative Group

Study: Final Follow-Up Experience of 8.5 Years," *Journal of the American Medical Association* 233 (1975): 872-77.

[4]Carl E. Thoreson and Lynda H. Powell, "Type A Behavior Pattern: New Perspectives on Theory, Assessment and Intervention," *Journal of Consulting and Clinical Psychology* 60 (1992): 595-604; Howard S. Friedman, Judith A. Hall and Monica J. Harris, "Type A Behavior, Nonverbal Expressive Style and Health," *Journal of Personality and Social Psychology* 48 (1985): 1299-315.

[5]Neil B. Rappaport, David P. McAnulty and Phillip J. Brantley, "Exploration of the Type A Behavior Pattern in Chronic Headache Sufferers," *Journal of Consulting and Clinical Psychology* 56 (1988): 621-23.

[6]Alexander Pope, quoted in *Contemporary Psychology* 37 (1992): 921.

[7]Dallas Willard, *The Spirit of the Disciplines* (San Francisco: HarperCollins, 1988), p. 4.

[8]William L. Hathaway, "The Religious Dimensions of Coping: Implications for Prevention and Promotion," *Prevention in Human Services* 9 (1991): 65-92; David R. Williams et al., "Religion and Psychological Distress in a Community Sample," *Social Science Medicine* 32 (1991): 1257-62; Harold G. Koenig, Linda K. George and Ilene C. Siegler, "The Use of Religion and Other Emotion-Regulating Coping Strategies Among Older Adults," *The Gerontologist* 28 (1988): 303-10.

[9]Richard Foster, *Celebration of Discipline: The Path to Spiritual Growth,* rev. ed. (San Francisco: Harper, 1988).

[10]Sheldon Cohen, "Psychosocial Models of the Role of Social Support in the Etiology of Physical Disease," *Health Psychology* 7 (1988): 269-97.

[11]James Pennebaker, *Opening Up: The Healing Power of Confiding in Others* (New York: William Morrow, 1990).

Chapter 6: Patience

[1]Stephen Eyre, *Patience: The Benefits of Waiting* (Grand Rapids, Mich.: Zondervan, 1991), p. 8.

[2]Martin E. P. Seligman, *Helplessness: On Depression, Development and Death* (San Francisco: Freeman, 1975).

[3]A. Kiester, "The Uses of Anger," *Psychology Today* 26 (July 1984).

[4]David G. Myers, *Psychology,* 3rd ed. (New York: Worth, 1992), p. 520.

[5]David Friend and editors of *Life* magazine, *The Meaning of Life* (Boston: Little, Brown, 1991), p. 90.

[6]Mark R. McMinn, "Mechanisms of Energy Balance in Obesity," *Behavioral Neuroscience* 98 (1984): 375-93.

[7]Kelly D. Brownell and Thomas A. Wadden, "Etiology and Treatment of Obesity: Understanding a Serious, Prevalent and Refractory Disorder," *Journal of Consulting and Clinical Psychology* 60 (1992): 505-17.

[8]Paul Brand with Philip Yancey, *Pain: The Gift Nobody Wants* (Grand Rapids, Mich.: Zondervan, 1993); Paul Brand with Philip Yancey, "And God Created Pain," *Christianity Today,* January 10, 1994, pp. 18-23.

[9]C. S. Lewis, *The Lion, the Witch and the Wardrobe* (New York: Macmillan, 1950), p. 113.

Chapter 7: Kindness
[1]John M. Drescher, *Spirit Fruit* (Scottdale, Penn.: Herald, 1974), p. 202.

[2]Stephen F. Winward, *Fruit of the Spirit* (Grand Rapids, Mich.: Eerdmans, 1981).

[3]Drescher, *Spirit Fruit.*

[4]Francis de Sales, quoted in ibid., p. 203.

[5]John M. Darley and Bibb Latane, "Bystander Intervention in Emergencies: Diffusion of Responsibility," *Journal of Personality and Social Psychology* 8 (1968): 377-83.

[6]Jeffrey H. Goldstein, *Social Psychology* (New York: Academic, 1980).

[7]Melvin J. Lerner and Carolyn H. Simmons, "Observer's Reaction to the Innocent Victim: Compassion or Rejection?" *Journal of Personality and Social Psychology* 4 (1966): 203-10.

[8]The name of the theory is social exchange theory. A more thorough explanation can be found in any introductory social psychology or sociology text.

[9]Robert S. Wyer, Galen V. Bodenhausen and Theresa F. Gorman, "Cognitive Mediators of Reactions to Rape," *Journal of Personality and Social Psychology* 48 (1985): 324-38.

[10]Steve Sjogren, *Conspiracy of Kindness* (Ann Arbor, Mich.: Servant, 1993).

[11]David G. Myers, *Psychology,* 3rd ed. (New York: Worth, 1992), p. 520.

[12]Lisa G. McMinn, "Social Responsibility and Christian Ethics," unpublished manuscript, 1994.

[13]Drescher, *Spirit Fruit,* p. 204.

Chapter 8: Generosity
[1]Einstein personally inscribed this quote on a picture he gave to Armand Hammer. The story is told in David Friend and editors of *Life* magazine, *The Meaning of Life* (Boston: Little, Brown, 1991), p. 29.

[2]John M. Drescher, *Spirit Fruit* (Scottdale, Penn.: Herald, 1974), p. 229.

[3]Robert C. Roberts, *The Sin of Greed and the Spirit of Christian Generosity* (Wheaton, Ill.: Wheaton College Center for Applied Ethics, 1994), p. 8.

[4]Stephen F. Winward, *Fruit of the Spirit* (Grand Rapids, Mich.: Eerdmans, 1981).

[5]Ibid., pp. 21-23.

[6]James D. Laird, "Self-Attribution of Emotion: The Effects of Expressive Behavior on the Quality of Emotional Experience," *Journal of Personality and Social Psychology* 29 (1974): 475-86.

[7]Fritz Strack, Leonard Martin and Sabine Stepper, "Inhibiting and Facilitating Conditions of the Human Smile: A Nonobtrusive Test of the Facial Feedback Hypothesis," *Journal of Personality and Social Psychology* 54 (1988): 768-77.

[8]Donald W. Hinze, *To Give and Give Again: A Christian Imperative for Generosity* (New York: Pilgrim, 1990), p. 1.

[9]Ronald H. Rottschafer, *The Search for Satisfaction: Getting More for Yourself and*

Giving More to Others (Grand Rapids, Mich.: Baker Book House, 1992), p. 107.

Chapter 9: Faithfulness
[1]Eugene H. Peterson, *A Long Obedience in the Same Direction: Discipleship in an Instant Society* (Downers Grove, Ill.: InterVarsity Press, 1980).
[2]This is called social exchange theory. For example, see George C. Homans, *Social Behavior: Its Elementary Forms* (New York: Harcourt, Brace and World, 1961); J. W. Thibaut and H. H. Kelley, *Interpersonal Relations* (New York: Wiley, 1978); J. S Adams, "Toward an Understanding of Inequity," *Journal of Abnormal and Social Psychology* 67 (1963): 422-36; E. Walster and G. W. Walster, *A New Look at Love* (Reading, Mass.: Addison-Wesley, 1978); U. G. Foa and E. B. Foa, *Societal Structures of the Mind* (Springfield, Ill.: Thomas, 1974).
[3]Suzanne M. Miller, Ellen R. Lack and Scott Asroff, "Preference for Control and Coronary-Prone Behavior Pattern: 'I'd Rather Do It Myself,' " *Journal of Personality and Social Psychology* 49 (1985): 492-99.
[4]John M. Drescher, *Spirit Fruit* (Scottdale, Penn.: Herald, 1974), p. 270.
[5]Kenneth J. Gergen, "The Effects of Interaction Goals and Personalistic Feedback on the Presentation of Self," *Journal of Personality and Social Psychology* 1 (1965): 413-24; Robert T. Croyle and Joel Cooper, "Dissonance Arousal: Physiological Evidence," *Journal of Personality and Social Psychology* 45 (1983): 782-91.
[6]David G. Myers, *Psychology*, 2nd ed. (New York: Worth, 1989), p. 560.
[7]Anthony Ryle, *Cognitive-Analytic Therapy: Active Participation in Change* (New York: Wiley, 1990).

Chapter 10: Gentleness
[1]Stephen F. Winward, *Fruit of the Spirit* (Grand Rapids, Mich.: Eerdmans, 1981).
[2]John M. Drescher, *Spirit Fruit* (Scottdale, Penn.: Herald, 1974), p. 285.
[3]Norma Haan, *Coping and Defending: Processes of Self-Environment Organization* (New York: Academic, 1977).
[4]Redford B. Williams Jr., John C. Barefoot and Richard B. Shekelle, "The Health Consequences of Hostility," in *Anger and Hostility in Cardiovascular and Behavioral Disorders*, ed. Margaret A. Chesney and Ray H. Rosenman (New York: McGraw-Hill, 1985); R. Williams, *The Trusting Heart: Great News About Type A Behavior* (New York: Random House, 1989).
[5]Cited by Leonard Berkowitz, "The Case for Bottling Up Rage," *Psychology Today*, July 1973, pp. 24-31.
[6]David G. Myers, *Psychology*, 3rd ed. (New York: Worth, 1992), p. 520.
[7]Cited in Martin Bolt, *Instructor's Resources* (New York: Worth, 1989).
[8]Charles D. Spielberger et al., "The Experience and Expression of Anger," in *Anger and Hostility in Cardiovascular and Behavioral Disorders*, ed. Margaret A. Chesney and Ray H. Rosenman, eds. (New York: McGraw-Hill, 1985).
[9]Helen Taylor and Cary L. Cooper, "The Stress-Prone Personality: A Review of the Research in the Context of Occupational Stress," *Stress Medicine* 5 (1989): 17-27.
[10]Phillip J. O'Connor, "Faith Helped Teacher Deal with Charges," *Chicago Sun-*

Notes

Times, May 19, 1994, p. 20.

[11]"Hey, I'm Terrific!" *Newsweek,* February 17, 1992, pp. 46-51.

[12]Richard J. Herrnstein and Charles Murray, *The Bell Curve: Intelligence and Class Structure in American Life* (New York: Free Press, 1994).

[13]Art Hilgart, "The U.Q. Test for Success," *The Nation,* November 21, 1994, p. 614.

[14]James J. Lynch, *The Language of the Heart: The Body's Response to Human Dialogue* (New York: Basic Books, 1985).

[15]Niall Bolger et al., "Effects of Daily Stress on Negative Mood," *Journal of Personality and Social Psychology* 57 (1989): 808-18; Lauren Schwartz, Mark A. Slater and Gary R. Birchler, "Interpersonal Stress and Pain Behaviors in Patients with Chronic Pain," *Journal of Consulting and Clinical Psychology* 62 (1994): 861-64.

[16]Andrew G. Billings and Rudolf H. Moos, "Life Stressors and Social Resources Affect Posttreatment Outcomes Among Depressed Patients," *Journal of Abnormal Psychology* 94 (1985): 140-53; Ralph W. Swindle Jr., Ruth C. Cronkite and Rudolf H. Moos, "Life Stressors, Social Resources, Coping and the Four-Year Course of Unipolar Depression," *Journal of Abnormal Psychology* 98 (1985): 468-77.

Chapter 11: Self-Control

[1]Art Golab, " 'Miracle Baby' Home," *Chicago Sun-Times,* May 19, 1994, p. 6.

[2]A. C. Green, "Faithful on and off the Court," *Decision,* March 1994, pp. 4-5.

[3]Kenneth S. Pope, Barbara G. Tabachnick and Patricia Keith-Speigel, "Ethics of Practice: The Beliefs and Behaviors of Psychologists as Therapists," *American Psychologist* (1987): 993-1006.

[4]Mark R. McMinn and Katheryn Rhoads Meek, "Ethics Among Christian Counselors: A Survey of Beliefs and Behaviors," *Journal of Psychology and Theology,* in press.

[5]I have described this in more detail in three other places: Mark R. McMinn, *Your Hidden Half* (Grand Rapids, Mich.: Baker Book House, 1988); *Dealing with Desires You Can't Control* (Colorado Springs: NavPress, 1990); *The Jekyll-Hyde Syndrome: Controlling Inner Conflict Through Authentic Living* (Newberg, Ore.: Barclay, forthcoming).

[6]Keith Humphreys, "Psychotherapy and the Twelve Step Approach for Substance Abuse: The Limits of Integration," *Psychotherapy* 30 (1993): 207-13.

[7]Robert N. Sollod, "Reply to Humphreys: On the Compatibility of Twelve-Step Programs and Psychotherapy," *Psychotherapy* 31 (1994): 549-50; Marilyn Freimuth, "Psychotherapy and Twelve-Step Programs: A Commentary on Humphreys," *Psychotherapy* 31 (1994): 551-53.

[8]William W. Wells, *Welcome to the Family: An Introduction to Evangelical Christianity* (Downers Grove, Ill.: InterVarsity Press, 1979).

[9]Peter Kreeft, *Back to Virtue: Traditional Moral Wisdom for Modern Moral Confusion* (San Francisco: Ignatius, 1992), p. 21.

[10]*Newsweek,* November 28, 1994.

Chapter 12: Stress & Redemption

[1]R. Allen and D. Hyde, *Investigations in Stress Control* (Minneapolis: Burgess,

1980).

[2]"The Good Life: It Can Kill You," published by Blue Cross Blue Shield of Oregon.

[3]Peter Kreeft, *Back to Virtue: Traditional Moral Wisdom for Modern Moral Confusion* (San Francisco: Ignatius, 1992), p. 88.

[4]Max Lucado, *On the Anvil: Stories on Being Shaped into God's Image* (Wheaton, Ill.: Tyndale House, 1985), p. 42.